Conversations for Results
By Frank Binnendyk

Copyright Page

Conversations for Results:
Accelerating Performance through Conversations
By: Frank Binnendyk

ISBN: 13: 978-0692958049
Imprint: Independently published
Copyright: © 2017 Frank Binnendyk
Published by: Keystone Innovation LLC, Portland, OR
First Printing: September 2017

All rights reserved. No part of this book may be reproduced in any electronic or material means, including storage and retrieval systems, without permission in writing from the publisher, except by reviewers, who may quote brief passages in review.

Visit: Conversations4Results.com

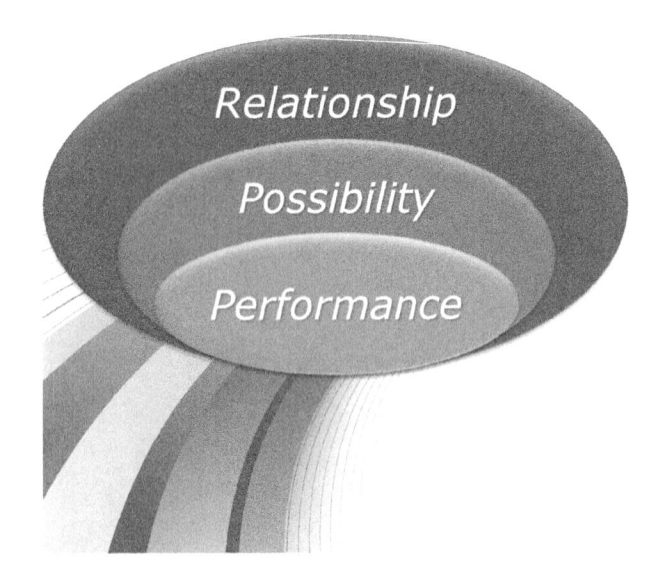

Acknowledgements

Many have contributed to this book both directly and indirectly. My wife Christine, a bestselling author herself, was generous with her edits and suggestions. Several of my six sisters were also kind in sharing their time and talent during the review period.

Several times in my career, I've been fortunate to find myself a member of an exceptionally high-performing business team. Many of the topics discussed in this book were born of the collaborative efforts of such a team at Cadence Design Systems', Executive College. Under the leadership of Spencer Clark and Leb Tannenbaum, an impressive team rallied to produce and deliver a series of world-class executive training programs. Key team members included: Dr. Rick Mirabile, Stewart Emery, Don Tyler, Dr. Dave Simpson, and Karen Howells. Thank you for the honor of working with each of you and the knowledge you shared!

Other authors have written on these topics and collectively influenced my thinking and practice. These include: Fernando Flores, Susan Scott, Kerry Patterson, M. Scott Peck, Chris Argyris, Dan Denison and Stephen Covey to name a few.

I would also like to acknowledge the hundreds of coaching clients who have put these tools to effective use and honored me with their praise and thanks. This book is for these and many future clients.

Sincerely,

Frank

Contents

Part 1 7

Chapter 1: Overarching principles: 7

Chapter 2: Set the Stage 8

   Signs the Stage isn't Set 8

   Pick the Venue 9

   Choose the Participants 10

   Analyze Stakeholders 10

   Choose your Mindset 11

   Create a safe environment 13

Chapter 3: Show Up in the Conversation 16

   Be Present 17

   Be Intentional 18

   Come Out from Behind Yourself 18

Chapter 4: Manage your Mindset 20

   Manage Your Internal Conversations 28

   Listen 34

   Be Direct 36

   Distinguish Facts from Meaning 39

   Manage Inferences 42

Chapter 5: Maintain Integrity 47

   Muster the courage 48

   Balance explaining and asking 49

   Be consistent in thoughts and actions 57

Chapter 6: Close the Loop 58

   Follow Through 59

   Confirm 59

   Tie-Off 60

Part 2 63
Chapter 7: Types of Conversations 63
Chapter 8: Conversations for Relationship 65
Rapport 65
Trust 70
Trust and Intimacy 74
Building Rapport 76
Group Rapport Building 78
Discovery 79
Relating 80
Agreement 81
Communication in Groups 81
Chapter 9: Conversations for Possibility: 86
Innovation Across an Organization 87
Ideation 87
Prioritization 92
Solution Selection 93
Enroll 95
Chapter 10: Conversations for Performance: 97
Building Blocks 98
Conversations for Action 101
Conversations for Delegation 112
Conversations for Accountability 114
Conversations for Confrontation 121
Conversations for Selling 133
Index 139

Preface

Improving conversations is your greatest lever for improving your business performance. We create everything in language, whether written, spoken, or gestured. When we communicate, we can give birth to new possibilities or accelerate ones already in existence. While poor communication can limit possibilities and crush dreams.

You choose how you present yourself in conversations. You have the choice of creating possibility and increasing your business velocity. Meaning both your speed and effectiveness.

This book provides tools and approaches to improve your skills in getting the results you desire. Without an enabling mindset, effective communication tools, and the skill to use them, you are working with a foundation that will not deliver your best outcome.

In this book, the author presents preconditions, theory, tools, and techniques that accelerate your business velocity.

The goal is for you to use this book as a "how-to" reference. Once you learn the overarching principles applicable to any conversation in Part 1, you will be able to go to specific sections in Part 2 to prepare for specific conversations where you want positive results.

An assumption in this book is that everyone has existing skills for conversations that get results. And, no individual is a finished product. We all have areas where we can improve. This improvement can either be in adding or refining conversation tools, or becoming more consistent in using them.

Part 1

Chapter 1: Overarching principles:

Set the stage
- Pick the venue
- Choose the participants
- Analyze stakeholders
- Choose your mindset
- Create a safe environment

Show up in the conversation
- Be present
- Be intentional with a desired outcome
- Come out from behind yourself

Manage your mindset
- Manage your internal conversation
- Listen
- Be direct
- Distinguish facts from meaning
- Manage inferences

Maintain integrity
- Muster courage
- Explain and ask
- Maintain consistency

Close the loop
- Follow through
- Confirm
- Tie-off

Chapter 2: Set the Stage

Set the stage
- Pick the venue
- Choose the participants
- Analyze stakeholders
- Choose your mindset
- Create a safe environment

To improve the velocity of your conversations it's best to intentionally **Set the Stage** for success. Occasionally, productive dialogue occurs without spending effort setting the stage. In those instances, you're leaving your possibility of success up to chance. When conversations matter, the wise will **Set the Stage**.

Louis Pasture reminds us that "chance favors the prepared mind." Or as the British Army adage goes "Proper planning and preparation prevents piss poor performance."

Signs the Stage isn't Set

- Have you ever found yourself thinking or saying, "this isn't the time or right place for this conversation?"
- Have you felt concerned that there isn't a quorum of the right participants for a productive conversation?
- When you're in meetings do you know all the people and what's important to them individually?
- Do you ever find that you're not ready for a conversation because you're mad, upset or

Chapter 2: Set the Stage

distracted by other thoughts and concerns in your day?
- Are you ever asked questions in meetings knowing it's not safe to speak your mind without incurring negative backlash?

If so, then you already have a clear idea of the impact of not setting the stage properly before a conversation.

Pick the Venue

Where you hold a conversation matters. For many conversations, the surroundings affect the quality of the conversation. Consider that it's different having a sensitive conversation in the following locations:

- Called into your boss' office
- Your boss coming into your office
- In a crowded room before another meeting starts
- While taking a stroll in nature on neutral ground

Think of the outcome you want and the most appropriate setting before calling your meeting.
- When posting and prioritizing ideas during brainstorming sessions (Conversations for Possibilities), rooms that provide lots of white boards or wall space for idea capturing and processing aid in getting higher quality results. Securing and preparing the room prior to your session will improve your odds of success.
- When conducting discovery conversations with customers, you will gain a deeper understanding by visiting the customer in their native environment.

9

- Use private versus public spaces for conversations of reprimand, while conversations for praise are fine in a more public setting.

Choose the Participants

For one-on-one meetings it is easy and obvious who to choose as participants. If the conversation has legal ramifications include a qualified third-party, like someone from the legal or human resources department.

Choosing participants becomes more important when you're working on issues that cross organizational boundaries. In these cases, there are many potential stakeholders and it's important to include those stakeholders or their trusted representatives. A good question to ask yourself when looking for stakeholders is "if excluded, who could potentially derail the outcome of this conversation?"

Analyze Stakeholders

Once you've listed all the potential stakeholders, review the list, and identify specific interests each of these stakeholders have in the outcome of your conversation. Consider issues like:

- Benefits to the stakeholders
- Required changes impacting the stakeholders
- Activities that might cause damage or conflict for stakeholders

Be able to answer two primary questions: "what's at stake for this individual?" and "what would this individual consider a win?"

Consider the likelihood that a stakeholder will have a negative response in this conversation. Assign a rating for how important this stakeholder is in affecting the outcome of your conversation. Pay special attention to those stakeholders who are most important to your desired outcome.

Choose your Mindset

We all experience different moods and motivations. Check your mindset before going into a conversation. You're going to get different results going in open-minded looking to discover versus going in closed-minded and looking for blame, retribution, or revenge.

Here is an experiment to show how your thoughts influence your physiology. Michel-Eugene Chevreul, a well-known French natural scientist from the 1830's, designed the experiment Chevreaul's Pendulum. He found that if you imagine something intensely, the human body behaves as if the imagined situation has already happened.

The experiment is very simple.

The experiment setup

Take a piece of paper and draw a circle 8 to 10 inches diameter. Make a cross in the center of the circle, then mark A at the top of the, C at the bottom. B to the right and D to the left of the circle where the cross intersects the circle

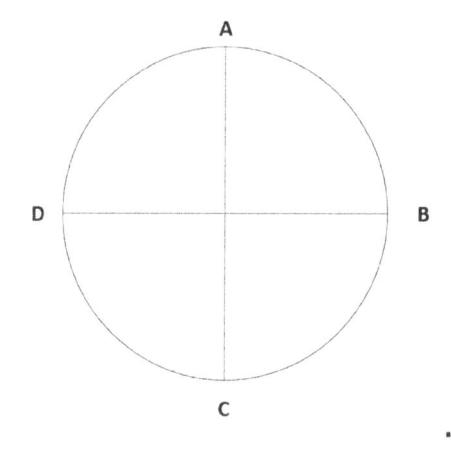

Take a piece of thread or floss (10 to 14 Inches). Attach a small weight (about 1g or less) a few paper clips or a small ring will be fine. Rest your elbow on the tabletop. Hold the thread between your thumb and forefinger so that the pendulum weight (paper clip or ring) hangs straight down ¼" to ¾" above the center of the circle. Hold the pendulum as still as possible.

The power of your mindset

Now comes the fun part. While holding the pendulum as still as possible, try to IMAGINE how it would feel if the pendulum started to swing vertically. Don't do anything to make it swing, just IMAGINE intensely, if the pendulum were, against all expectations, to start swinging all by itself. After 15 seconds to 2 minutes of intense imagining the pendulum starts swinging, at first with small swings and then these soon grow to wide, bold swings in the vertical direction.

When you have succeeded with the vertical swings, imagine what it would feel like if the pendulum started rotating clockwise. Think ABCD, ABCD. Once again, your mind influences the pendulum and it starts rotating in the way you imagined.

When you image the pendulum swinging, your body subconsciously makes very small, almost imperceptible movements in the proper direction. A pendulum is an energy accumulating system, so imperceptible swings quickly add up.

Likewise, the thoughts you have going into and during a conversation affect how you show up in the conversation and have an impact on the outcome.

When we use the term "show up", we refer to how you present yourself in the conversation.

To what degree are you:
Offering your input or holding back?
Assertive or reserved?
Emotional or calm?
Accepting or defensive?
Mentally present or distracted and vacant?
Fidgety or attentive?

Create a safe environment

Holding conversations with agreed-upon ground rules creates a safety net. My business partner tells a compelling story about going to visit the Russian circus in Moscow. One of the acts was a high wire trapeze routine. The throws and catches were spellbinding. Then at one point, the ringmaster orders to have the safety net removed. The result was a gasp from the audience in realizing that one slip, one missed catch could result in the death of an individual. It was at that point that he chose to get up and leave the performance and not be part of such an event. His amusement was not worth the risk of someone's life. He uses the story in beginning of meetings where individuals are going to speak from the heart and divulge information that creates vulnerability. He asks the participant to extend a safety net in the form of ground rules so that everyone remains safe and can fully participate.

The following question is key for establishing ground rules in group meetings. "What conditions need to be present in this room for you to fully participate?" Some typical ground rules include:

- What's said in the room stays in the room, unless there is express permission to do otherwise
- One person speaks at a time
- No personal attacks, it is OK to challenge ideas and reasoning but not the character of the individual

Not all ground rules form the safety net. Other procedural ground rules include items like:

- Cell phones off
- Start, stop, and return from breaks on time
- No side conversations

- Paraphrase what you've just heard before weighing in with your own opinion
- Don't avoid the tough conversations, have the courage to get the challenging words across the threshold of your lips

Even for one-on-one meetings, it's important to clarify the conditions of confidentiality. If you intend to share the content of the meeting, indicate this before the meeting starts.

Keep in mind that violating ground rules is a serious breach of integrity and should meet with equally profound consequences. Keeping confidences is a characteristic of a trusted relationship and trust is the foundation for building a solid productive work environment. Trust is fragile, easily broken, and tough to rebuild.

Of course, you will inevitably find yourself in conversations where no safety net is present. It is very difficult or even foolish to fully show up in the conversation when it's not a safe environment. At those times, take it upon yourself, even if you're not the leader, to create the conditions necessary for you to fully participate. This may require you to muster some courage.

Chapter 3: Show Up in the Conversation

Set the stage
- Pick the venue
- Choose the participants
- Analyze stakeholders
- Choose your mindset
- Create a safe environment

Show up in the conversation
- Be present
- Be intentional with a desired outcome
- Come out from behind yourself

To improve the velocity of your conversations you need to fully participate in the conversation. Here are some reasons you may not be showing up well in conversations:

- Have you ever found yourself in a meeting and your body was there but your mind was somewhere else?
- Ever caught yourself thinking about something else, in the past or something in the future instead of the words in the conversation?
- Have you ever been sitting in a meeting wondering "where is this going?" or "when is this going to end?"
- Have you ever been sitting in a meeting knowing there was a topic that needed addressing but something was holding you back from opening your mouth and inserting it into the conversation?

Chapter 3: Show Up in the Conversation

Remember, the most important time is now. The most important person is the one you're currently talking to. The most important thing to do in the conversation is fully participate. Listening, really listening is a gift to the other person.

The presence of ground rules and a safety net are reasonable preconditions for you to participate in a conversation. Ensure you set the stage properly before engaging in conversation. This will allow you to continue with safety and confidence.

Be Present

Being present in a conversation is about focusing your attention on the conversation. Being present isn't simply about arriving on time, although that is a good start. It's more about being mentally present and able to attend emotionally in the moment. If your body is in the room but your mind is off dealing with some event that happened to you earlier or it's running through things you need to prepare for the future, then you're not fully present.

A quote from the cartoonist Bil Keane is an appropriate for being present "Yesterday is history, tomorrow is a mystery, today is a gift of God, which is why we call it the present." If a conversation is worth having, then it is worth giving your full time and attention.

It's human nature to dwell on the past and to think about the future. Pay attention to <u>when</u> that's happening during the conversation. Re-presence

17

yourself by focusing on the words the other person is saying and the true meaning they're trying to convey. If that is unclear to you, ask clarifying questions to help bring yourself back into the moment.

It's very generous to be present during a conversation. It's even more generous to be present in a space of love and caring, even in business conversations.

Be Intentional with a Desired Outcome in Mind

Being intentional and having a clear desired outcome prior to beginning the conversation leads to showing up well in the conversation. Even if you don't know the outcome in advance, part of your intentions can be:

- Leaving the conversation having put all the issues on the table
- Not compromising personal values
- Not holding back the truth, as spoken from a space of love and caring. Speaking the truth in love and caring is the opposite of speaking the truth with a mean vindictive bite.

Come Out from Behind Yourself

Sometimes, we lack the courage to face a strong personality participating with us in a conversation. This can lead to hiding behind yourself and limiting what you're capable of, by not fully weighing in with your point of view.

Keep the underlying principle of the discussion topic in your mind and be a champion for that principle. This technique can emancipate the energy you need to fully engage in the conversation. As Rollo May tells us, "the opposite of courage in our society is not cowardice, it is conformity".

The idea of "going along to get along" allows us to hide behind ourselves. In some cases, the consequences of holding back are of little importance and the reality is that it may not make a substantial difference on an individual basis. Another theory suggests that the effects of holding back are cumulative and eventually reach a tipping point. Beyond the tipping point the risk to your desired outcomes and your personal growth increases by orders of magnitude. A key question to ask yourself is "Am I showing up as part of the problem or as part of the solution?" In most cases hiding behind yourself makes you part of the problem.

You will accelerate your performance if you identify what's holding you back in the conversations and muster the courage to confront it. Often, some underlying fear, that may or may not be real, holds you back. It is possible to confront that fear. It is up to you to identify fear and begin to confront it.

"When you use your fear, it can take you to the place where you store your courage" - Amelia Earhart

Chapter 4: Manage your Mindset

Set the stage
- Pick the venue
- Choose the participants
- Analyze stakeholders
- Choose your mindset
- Create a safe environment

Show up in the conversation
- Be present
- Be intentional with a desired outcome
- Come out from behind yourself

Manage your mindset
- Manage your internal conversation
- Listen
- Be direct
- Distinguish facts from meaning
- Manage inferences

- Have you ever found yourself so caught up in your own internal dialogue that you've missed important points the other person was making?
- Have you ever come home from work and had your kids greet you immediately with something they think is important but find yourself thinking about what was going on at work earlier and not really listen to them?
- Have you ever avoided saying something directly to an individual because you might hurt their feelings?
- Do you ever find yourself overreacting emotionally to something said in innocence?
- Do you ever find yourself jumping to conclusions?

Chapter 4: Manage your Mindset

If you answered yes to any or all the above questions, rest assured that you're in good company. These are challenges we all face. The good news is managing your mindset can address these challenges.

If we express results as an equation, it might look like the following:

Results = f (Mindset) x (Conversations) x (Mechanisms)

For purposes of focusing our attention in this book, we are not going to explore mechanisms and will simplify the equation. If we did explore mechanisms, we would be looking at things like: organizational structure; technology; policies; competencies; skills; business process; information management systems; project management; research and development; organizational development; and behavior.

To make this useful we will simplify the equation with the following representative lists (by no means exhaustive) under the headings of mindset and conversations.

Results = f (Mindset)   x   (Conversations)

Mindset	*Conversations*
Attitude	*Relationship*
Intention	*Possibility*
Accountability	*Performance*
Responsibility	
Energy	
Enthusiasm	
Commitment	
Spirit	
Edge	
Creativity	
Imagination	
Thinking	

21

Notice that the equation contains a multiplier. Having a conversation while holding onto a bad attitude or intention will seriously impact the results. You must not only choose the right words in a conversation, you also need to choose your mindset.

Some mindsets powerfully take you in positive directions. Negative or destructive mindsets place you as a major part of the problem and totally undermine positive results.

Our mindset is something we choose. At times, many of us feel like we don't have that choice, we are the victim of circumstances and justified in our poor attitude. When these thoughts emerge, reflect on the positive attitude of some people facing life's most challenging conditions. Think of the cancer patient with a positive attitude and a mantra of "I have cancer, but cancer does not have me". If these inspirational individuals can choose their mindset, then certainly you have the ability to choose yours.

Consider the impact of shifting from a mindset of being the best in the world to being the best for the world.

Your mental framework has an enormous impact on results. There are three basic mental frameworks that come into play. The first is an assertive **Take Control** frame. The second is an unassertive, passive **Give Up Control** frame. The third is a **Mutual Learning** frame.

Take Control frame

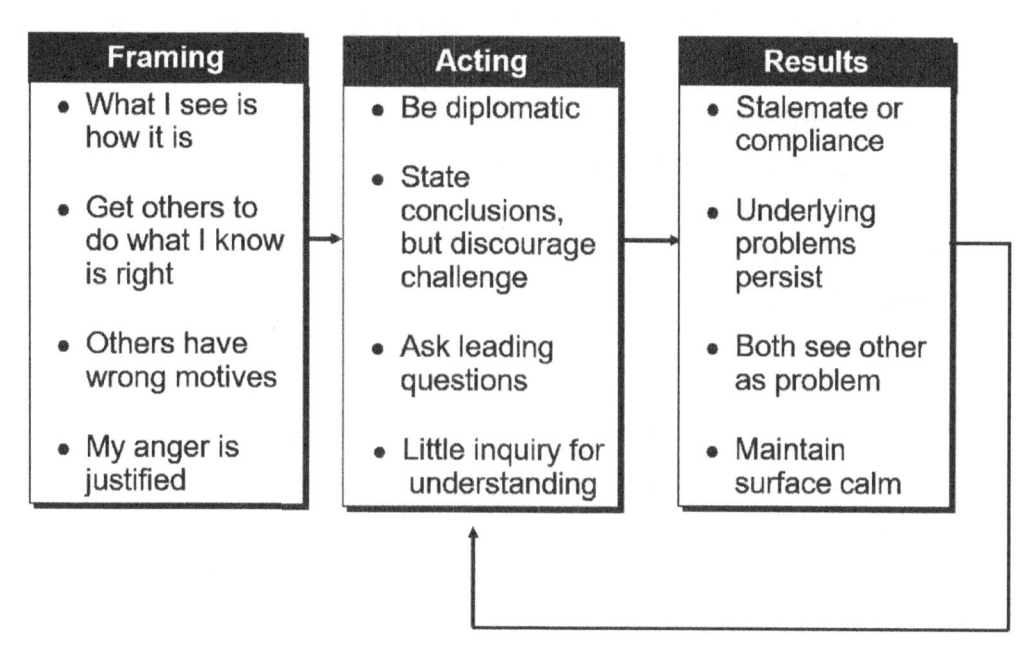

Framing	Acting	Results
• What I see is how it is	• Be diplomatic	• Stalemate or compliance
• Get others to do what I know is right	• State conclusions, but discourage challenge	• Underlying problems persist
• Others have wrong motives	• Ask leading questions	• Both see other as problem
• My anger is justified	• Little inquiry for understanding	• Maintain surface calm

The **Take Control frame** shown above can have appropriate uses when applied in the right context. For example, a military commander in a battle situation may need to exercise a command and control style of leadership to get the desired results and preserve the lives of those under his command.

In the **Take Control frame**, the leader believes their way of seeing the situation is the way it is. They tend to take unilateral control while believing they are right and sensible. The attitude is win and don't lose. They believe their role consists of getting others to do what they know is right and if others go against their directive, then the other person has the wrong motives and justifies the leader's anger. They practice saving face.

Someone acting in the **Take Control frame** asserts their views. They might be diplomatic, however if it's a life-and-death situation, they set aside diplomacy in favor of immediate results. The speaking and action show up as stating conclusions and discourages any challenge. The few questions asked, lead the other parties to respond in favor of how the take control individual sees the world. There is little if any questioning to gain additional understanding.

The results achieved from this frame during critical life-and-death situations lead to quick and appropriate compliance. In non-critical situations, there may be a stalemate at best. In either case, if there are underlying problems, then they still exist.

Some individuals remain stuck in the **Take Control frame**. Even if they don't get the results they're looking for, they continue to rely on the same types of actions.

Chapter 4: Manage your Mindset

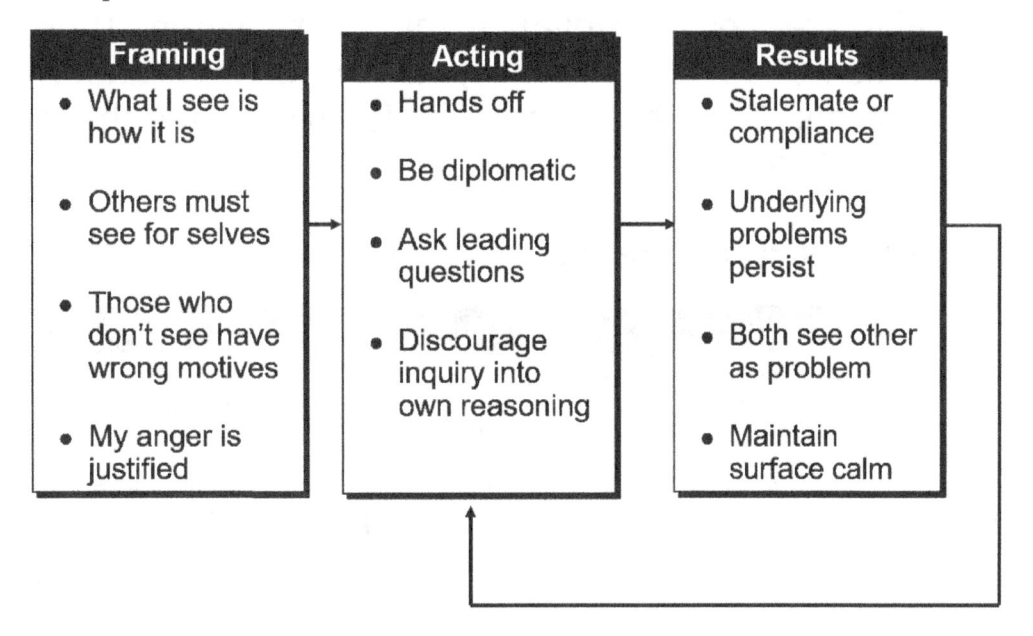

Give Up Control frame

Framing	Acting	Results
• What I see is how it is • Others must see for selves • Those who don't see have wrong motives • My anger is justified	• Hands off • Be diplomatic • Ask leading questions • Discourage inquiry into own reasoning	• Stalemate or compliance • Underlying problems persist • Both see other as problem • Maintain surface calm

The **Give Up Control frame** is more typical of people who are nonassertive and avoid conflict. In the **Give Up Control frame**, individuals also believe that the way they see situations are the way they really exist. Instead of trying to get others to see the world as they do, they often behave as if others need to see the situation for themselves. The give up control individual thinks of those who don't see the situation the same way as having the wrong motives. The give up control individual presumes justification in any anger they experience.

The way the Give Up Control individual acts is by being hands off. They may also be diplomatic. They may tend to ask leading questions and discourage inquiry for additional understanding.

The results achieved from this model often leads to a stalemate, or compliance at best, when there is conflict. In either case, if there are underlying problems then they still exist, even though things seem calm on the surface.

Mutual Learning frame

Framing	Acting	Results
• Each may see what others miss • Use differences to improve • Others strive to act with integrity • I may be contributing to difficulty	• Exchange all relevant information • Explain my view • Ask for other views • Make dilemmas discussible	• Informed choice and commitment • Act on shared concerns • Underlying problems addressed • Each feels understood and respected

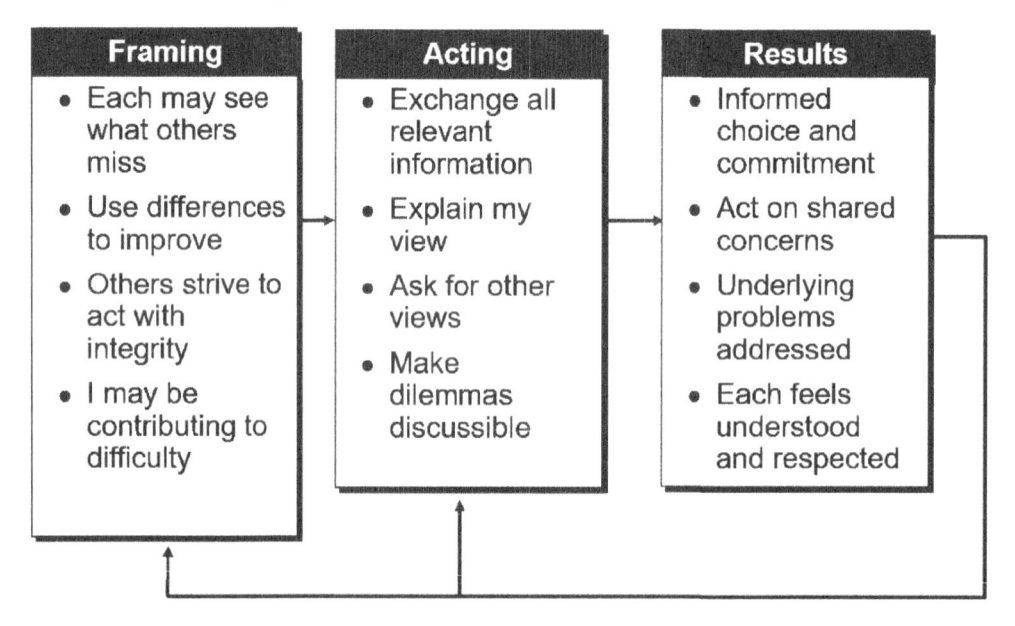

The Mutual Learning frame is the most powerful in supporting conversations for results. The mindset in the Mutual Learning frame is that each person in the conversation may see what the other person misses. They use those differences to improve and to learn. Each strives to act with integrity. And when things don't go right, they ask themselves how they may be contributing to the problem or difficulty.

When acting, those using the **Mutual Learning frame** focus on exchanging all relevant information.

Chapter 4: Manage your Mindset

They typically do this by explaining their view and the rationale behind that view and then asking others for their viewpoint and their rationale. When everyone has a chance to speak and everyone listens, dilemmas become discussable instead of the group engaging in finger pointing.

The results stemming from a mutual learning model include making informed and committed choices. The participants act on shared concerns. This approach enables fixing underlying problems. This in turn, leads to future success. At the end of the conversation, when following the **Mutual Learning frame**, each of the participants feel understood and respected.

You will notice that there is a second arrow going up to the framing box in the **Mutual Learning frame**. This arrow highlights the double-loop learning process. The principle behind double-loop learning is that if you act and repeatedly get results that are unsatisfactory, then you need to loop back and re-examine your frame to see if there's one more appropriate for the situation.

Some useful guidelines for changing your mindset include:
- assume that the other person acts with integrity and good motives
- remain curious about others' thinking
- ask open ended questions to get a firm understanding

Chapter 4: Manage your Mindset

- look for dilemmas that others may face and raise dilemmas that you experience
- assume both parties are contributing to any difficulty
- assume you may be missing things others see, and seeing things others miss

Our mindset influences: where we focus, what we 'see', how we interpret what we see, our actions, and our results.

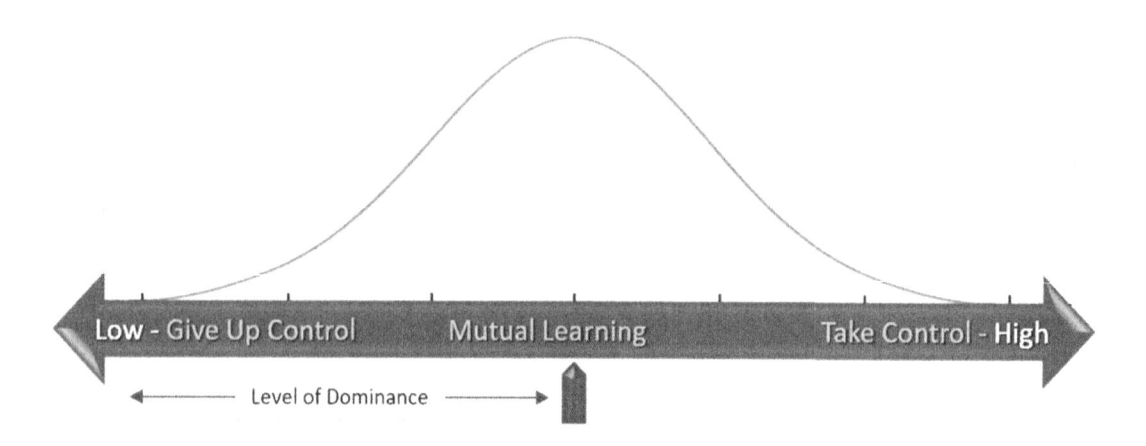

![Bell curve diagram showing a spectrum with "Low - Give Up Control" on the left, "Mutual Learning" in the center, and "Take Control - High" on the right, with "Level of Dominance" indicated below.]

There are appropriate times for operating in both the **Give-up Control** and **Take Control** frames. However, typical business managers should spend most of their time in the **Mutual Learning Frame.**

Manage Your Internal Conversations
When we're talking to someone, there are in fact two conversations going on. One is the explicit conversation that shows up in the spoken word. The other

Chapter 4: Manage your Mindset

conversation is the one that occurs in your brain and reflects what you're thinking and feeling but not saying. Your mindset governs the tone of your internal conversations. With practice, you will come to recognize your internal conversations and use them to make the external explicit conversation more productive leading to better results.

Peter Senge coined the phrase "left-hand column." Here is an exercise that illustrates the left-hand column.

Take a piece of paper and draw a line down the middle. Label the right-hand side (right-hand column) "what was spoken" and label the left side (left-hand column) "what I was thinking".

Next, think of a difficult conversation you recently had where you remember the back-and-forth dialogue. It doesn't have to be an extended conversation. It could just be a half a dozen sound-bites that transpired. Writing in as close to verbatim as possible, write what they said and write what you said in sequence. It's helpful to label the speaker for each of the sound-bites or sentences. After you have captured one or two paragraphs of verbatim conversation, shift your focus to what you were thinking while the conversation was going on. An example is on the next page.

Chapter 4: Manage your Mindset

What I was thinking (Left-hand)	What was spoken (Right-hand)
Don doesn't like to lose. Here he goes pushing personal views. We've had this conversation before.	Me: I don't understand why you have a problem with my suggestion.
If you're right we're already dead.	Don: Like I said this won't work. It will eventually get us in financial trouble.
	Me: It sounds like you want to do nothing. If we can't fix the business we might as well sell it.
That is just preying on the owner's fears. It might help if you offered ideas about how we could make this work.	Don: We've been through this before. Your proposal is too risky.
	Me: I'm not saying there's no risk; I'm saying that doing nothing is not the answer. Your team was there when we made the plan and they didn't see it as that big a risk.
The hell I did! I asked for their opinions.	Don: You were a steamroller and just pushed your ideas through. They said they tried to bring up the risks but you wouldn't listen.
	(and so on. . .)

Your left-hand column is a powerful insight into your thinking and your mindset. It says more about you and how you look at the situation than anything else. Your left-hand column can be a valuable resource for learning. However, if you don't pay attention, it becomes an obstacle. The following are steps to improve your left-hand column when in a tough conversation.

Take responsibility for your reactions. Keep in mind that you're looking at the conversation through your own filters and biases as influenced by your own mindset. You're reacting to what other people say from your perspective, shaped by your own personal biases and limited point of view. Notice what you're experiencing and be curious about your reactions. Suspend quick judgements about whether the other person is right or wrong. You might say to yourself: "I'm really upset. This is more about me. What about this exchange is upsetting me?"

Realize you select data. In a conversation, it is common for people to look for bits of data that support their pre-existing ideas. Consciously or not, you're selecting what data to focus on and what data to ignore. The context of the conversation and your mindset further influence the selection process. Ask yourself: "Which part of what I've heard am I reacting to? Did I miss something important?"

Paraphrase the meaning. Once aware of your data selection, it is useful to put into your own words (silently) what the person is saying or doing. Be aware of the key logic or intention in their view. Ask yourself: "if I assume they have good intentions, is there an alternate meaning that makes sense?"

Label what is happening. Once you understand the logic or intention of the person's view, use tools such as the Ladder of Inference, and Explaining and Asking (discussed later in this book) to describe the person's actions. This may help you determine whether data or reasoning is missing that could help you understand how they came to their conclusions. For example, rather than saying to yourself, "he is being so defiant!" you might say, "he is explaining that hiring temporary staff will make our problems worse, but he hasn't said what leads him to that conclusion".

Operate from a mutual learning model. Avoid making guarded or self-protective judgements. Instead of assuming others are to blame and that they act with bad intentions, you could think to yourself: "they may see this differently because they have data I don't". "If we make our reasoning explicit we can make an informed choice". "What am I doing that may contribute to this difficulty?"

Instruct yourself to advance mutual learning. Left unchecked, people's left-hand column often goes negative. Instead, give yourself proactive instructions to increase mutual learning. For example, tell yourself, "I need to ask him what he has seen or heard, or what he thinks will happen, that lead him to that conclusion.

Clear the cache. Pay attention to the volume and intensity of your left-hand column. At times, it can totally get in the way of hearing what the other person is trying to communicate. Clear out your left-hand column by appropriately and explicitly, express those thoughts in the right-hand column as part of the conversation. Not all of what goes on in your left-hand column is appropriate to share. You be the judge. When the other person understands the concept of the left-hand column a shorthand technique can be to say, "I have a left-hand column building and it is getting in the way of me fully understanding you. Do you mind if we talk about that for a moment so that I can clear it and better understand your position?"

In a group situation, people understand the idea of the left-hand column quickly. Within minutes they can be saying to each other, "I've got a left-hand column on that one". In using the "left-hand column" label, people give themselves permission to say things they would usually not say. This way, more of the significant issues get into the conversation.

Common Pitfalls
The risk is that while people can choose to reveal more of their left-hand column, they may not have the skills to tactfully do so. Getting more of the significant issues on the table may be a problem if people lack the time and skills to address them properly. When people engage without using skills, it's possible for them to become defensive or say unforgivable things.

Here are some useful guidelines to keep in mind.

- The proper use of the left-hand column is not that people should blurt out everything they think and feel. Rather, become more aware of what's left unsaid and to consider how to raise the unspoken issues productively.

- It is okay to disclose some left-hand column thoughts and feelings while choosing not to reveal others.

Chapter 4: Manage your Mindset

- Each of us are responsible for what we choose to disclose and keep private.
- Your left-hand column says more about you than it says about others. Use it to get perspective on your own mindset by observing yourself having thoughts and feelings.
- When we believe we are having unspeakable thoughts and feelings, we usually assume that others are the problem, we attribute nasty motives to them, and believe these to be obvious. Change this mindset by assuming good intentions and productive conversation becomes much more likely.
- Offer your left-hand column as an object to be reflected upon ("The thoughts going through my mind are…. Let's see, what triggered that?") rather than being judging or accusing.
- Groups may need a neutral facilitator to help turn left-hand column disclosures into productive conversation.

Listen

On the road to creating velocity through conversations for results, listening is the superhighway.

Listening and hearing are two different things. You may be hearing someone's words but if you're not willing to let these words influence your thinking, then you're not really listening.

When we listen to someone talk, our default is paying more attention to the side-conversation (left-hand column) we have in our own mind. We internally filter what we hear, see, and feel during the exchange.

What counts for communication is more than what we hear. Tone, verbal cues, and emotions influence it. Although experts debunked the myth that 93% of communication is nonverbal, the amount of non-verbal influence is still significant.

The Japanese Kanji symbol for listening elegantly brings these dimensions together. The individual symbols that form the composite "to listen" include: Ear, King (Unity between Heaven, Man, and Earth), You, Eye, Undivided Attention, and Heart.

聽

Ear
King
You
Eye
Undivided Attention
Heart

When you listen, give the person speaking cues that you're with them. Do this passively by taking an open posture and maintaining eye contact, offering simple acknowledgments, and otherwise remaining silent. Another more engaging approach is active listening. When we actively listen, we are taking in what the speaker says, waiting for a natural break, and then reflecting what it is we're hearing. To do this, repeat what you heard into your own summary. When you become highly effective, reflect the feelings behind what the other person is saying. It is not a wise idea to simply parrot back the exact words. After a speaker hears their exact words repeated back verbatim a couple of times, they often become annoyed. This was a favorite way to torment my six sisters when I was young.

My best advice for being attentive when someone is speaking is: listen and be willing to "try-on" the concepts they are presenting. This means:

- accepting what the speaker says, even if you disagree
- not interrupting; but do use active listening
- suspend judgment for now
- ask open ended questions to get more detail
- focus your full attention

The hard part is putting this advice into action. This is because you have your own internal conversation going on while you're dealing with any emotional content in the communication. With practice and discipline, you will get good at it. Getting good involves making a conscious effort.

Be Direct

Being Direct presents a difficult challenge for many people. The difficulty often happens when you hold the mindset of not wanting to hurt another's feelings. Being indirect or avoid confrontation altogether is not doing others any favors.

Being direct is a skillset that is learnable. To do so, speak the truth from a space of love and caring. Although it may seem awkward to talk about love in a business environment, keep in mind that often the loving and caring thing to do is share information with another so they can improve. Sometimes that means being a wall of truth that others can press against and grow. If there's nothing to press against and there are no defined boundaries, it's very difficult for most people to self-correct.

Being Direct doesn't necessarily mean you need to be harsh or callous in your delivery. The more caring and thoughtful action is being open and honest while remaining empathetic and caring. When your delivery comes across as not caring about another's feelings, you also show up as untrustworthy. One of the foundations of trust is expressing empathy by means of having another's best interest at heart. When you speak the truth in love, be both direct and empathetically caring.

Hugo Mieth wrote that sometimes to be effective and get results you need to be a "practiced" jerk. His point is that some people without skills are jerks all the time and don't know how to turn it off. Someone practiced at this knows how to speak the truth. Even though it is a difficult message to deliver they can step-up to the challenge. This is what "practiced" means. In other words, the best way to be direct is be intentional.

Chapter 4: Manage your Mindset

Another way to look at it is that if you're a people pleaser and you avoid being direct, thinking you're sparing other's feelings, then you're paying a heavy personal price at each occurrence. Each time you hide your true self and feelings by not being direct, you lose a little of your own authenticity and sense of self. Lose too much, and recovery becomes extremely difficult. What you may find when you're direct is that people are more comfortable around you because they know where you stand and may in fact like you better.

The things that keep people from **Being Direct** include:

- Being afraid of conflict
- Fear of rejection, embarrassment or not being liked
- Fear of hurting somebody
- Fear of looking foolish by asking "dumb" questions
- The false hope that someone is going to magically know what we want and need without us voicing it

False beliefs about **Being Direct** include:

- you will always upset other people
- you will always appear selfish or arrogant
- you will always inconvenience other people by asking
- others will not like you

It is important to **Be Direct** because:

- it's honest, truthful and authentic;
- it demonstrates respect for yourself and for others;
- it saves yourself and others time, energy, and money;

- it promotes intimacy and trust.

Some suggestions for **Being Direct** include:

- Check in with how your body is reacting in terms of the feelings you're holding inside. Make sure they are consistent with what you're saying. If your feelings are so intense that you cannot speak diplomatically, give yourself the time to explore your feelings before speaking.
- Before you speak, ask yourself if what you're about to say is true, kind, and necessary. This will help you keep your ego in check and give you a buffer to help you stop from saying destructive statements out of anger
- Keep it simple, clear, and concise, as brief is better.
- Speak in terms of "I" rather than "you," as "you" statements often get a defensive reaction.
- Avoid "always" and "never" statements as they are embellishments that are rarely true. Those terms weaken your point and evoke a negative response
- Avoid complaining to a third-party; speak directly to the source rather than putting someone else in the middle.
- Be kind to yourself by saying "no" as needed and don't overpromise or overextend yourself.
- Whenever possible, replace the word "but" with "and.". When "but" occurs in a conversation it negates what's said just prior. "And" maintains the truth and integrity of what's stated while

productively adding on to it. Think of it as "both/and" versus "either/or".

Distinguish Facts from Meaning

Sometimes we inappropriately collapse facts with meaning, causing an emotional reaction for ourselves. For example, if someone gets called-out for missing a deadline, they may have a strong negative reaction because in their mind, they equate missing a deadline with being a bad person. So, when they hear you say they missed a deadline, what they interpret is: you're saying they're a bad person.

This happens in one degree or another to all of us. Most of the time we are not even aware it is happening.

Fix these misinterpretations by separating out **fact** from **meaning**. Make two lists. In one, write down all the observable or undisputed facts. In the second, write down the meanings that you're attaching to the facts. Start by writing the first meaning that comes to mind and then ask yourself could it mean something else. Repeat asking "could it mean anything else," until you've exhausted all the meanings that come to mind. Sometimes, it's helpful to think of it from another point of view:

- Sally, an optimist who sees the glass as half full: what might this mean to her?
- John, a pessimist who sees the glass as half empty: what meaning might he make of this fact?
- The creative Christine, who sees the glass as refillable, offers another perspective.

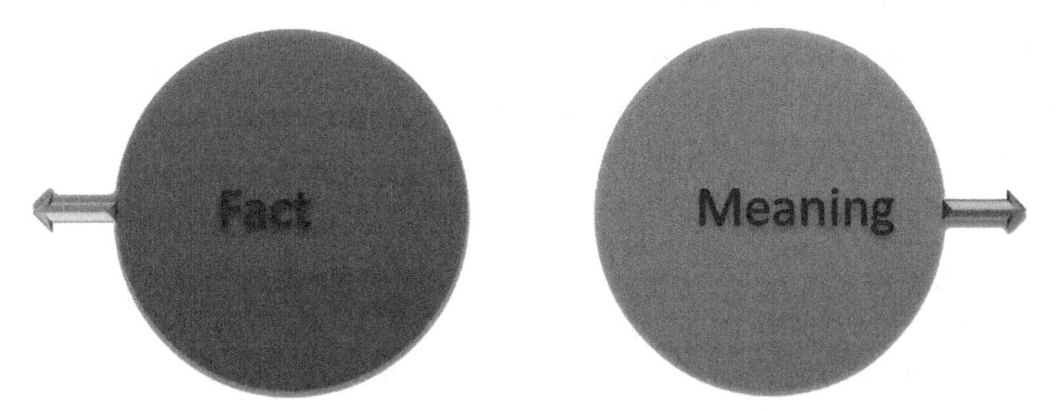

Fact: Someone missed a deadline. The meaning can be anything you want to assign as meaning. You can choose it to mean something positive, negative, or nothing at all. The reality is that facts do not have any meaning until we assign them and then, it is our choice.

When listening, sometimes phrases trigger your mind to assign emotional meaning yanking you around like an emotional yo-yo. For example, telling someone in an accounting or finance role that their work is inaccurate, or saying to someone in a marketing role that they are not creative, or saying to someone in HR that they don't get along well with people is likely to trigger a negative reaction. Learn to listen to the facts and suspend assigning meaning.

Try the exercise of distinguishing **facts** from **meaning** several times. The outcome from doing this exercise can be transformational. Once you habituate separating fact from meaning, events will be easier to understand for what they are and your life may feel a whole lot simpler and more in control.

Manage Inferences

The Managing Inferences technique is similar, but different from distinguishing facts from meaning. The following section on the Ladder of Inference is derived from the work of Argyris, Putnam and Smith.

Our brain is a huge connection engine. We are constantly making observations and selecting bits of data that influence our actions. Given any two lists and tasked with finding ways to connect the items in those lists, your brain will work very hard and effectively at creating connections.

In conversation, our brain will select a limited set of data from the pool of all data available. In our mind, we make assumptions and draw meaning from the data we have selected. From there we draw conclusions based on those assumptions and adopt beliefs. And in the last step we act based on our beliefs. An amazing thing about our brains is that this can all happen in a fraction of a second.

The Ladder of Inference

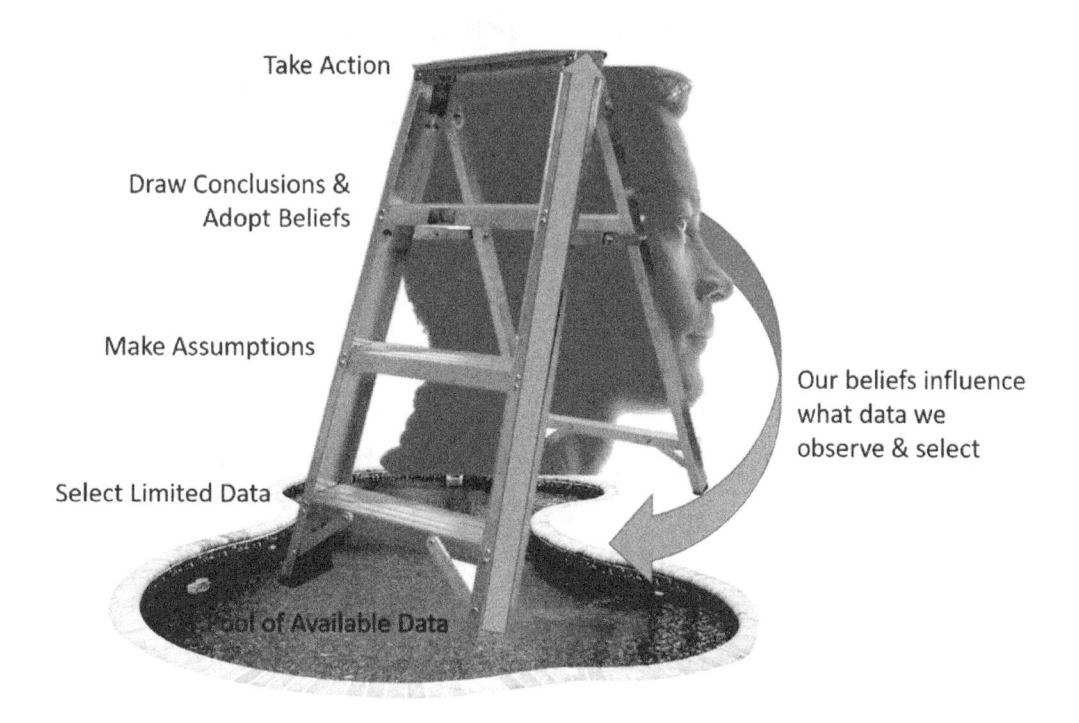

A problem occurs when we make assumptions and adopt beliefs with limited data. It's very easy and natural for us to make bad assumptions, adopt inaccurate beliefs, draw improper conclusions, and take inappropriate action. It happens all too often. This gets compounded when your existing beliefs influence what you observe and the data you select. This creates a reinforcing loop.

Further compounding occurs when past evidence indicates you got it right once in the past. Although it was right then, it may not be right now. For example, this person did me wrong in the past. My current observation leads me to believe it is happening again! The next thing you know, I am taking action with very little data and a lot of assumptions.

When you find yourself sprinting up the ladder of inference and suspect you're taking inappropriate action, stop, and expand the pool of data. Often, additional data points can set you on the right track.

To really examine your thinking, it's necessary to carefully step back down the ladder one rung at a time and challenge your choices at each rung. Ask yourself:

- What did I believe to be true that caused me to take that action?
- What conclusions did I draw that formed those beliefs?
- What assumptions was I making that led me to draw those conclusions?
- Could I form different conclusions by looking at more or different data?
- How can I expand the pool of data?

Questions to Ask	Ladder of Inference	Example
What action did I take based upon my beliefs?	**Actions**	I go.
What did I believe to be true that caused me to take that action?	**Beliefs**	I can go.
What conclusions did I draw that formed those beliefs?	**Conclusions**	I can trust the traffic light. I can trust others to follow the traffic light. I should obey the traffic light.
What assumptions was I making that led me to draw those conclusions?	**Assumptions**	The traffic light controls traffic.
What did I see/hear?	**Selected "Data"**	Black box with green light shining.
Data and experiences as a video tape recorder might capture it.	**Pool of Available Data**	Street scene with traffic including black box with red, yellow, and green lights. Cars to my right and left are stopped. The light facing me is green.

▓ = The Reinforcing Loop

Chapter 4: Manage your Mindset

When working through your reasoning, look for rungs in the ladder that you tend to jump. For example, do you tend to make assumptions too easily? Do you tend to select only part of the data? Note your tendencies so that you learn to do that step of reasoning with extra thought in the future.

Chapter 5: Maintain Integrity

Set the stage
- Pick the venue
- Choose the participants
- Analyze stakeholders
- Choose your mindset
- Create a safe environment

Show up in the conversation
- Be present
- Be intentional with a desired outcome
- Come out from behind yourself

Manage your mindset
- Manage your internal conversation
- Listen
- Be direct
- Distinguish facts from meaning
- Manage inferences

Maintain integrity
- Muster courage
- Explain and ask
- Maintain consistency

- After a conversation do you ever feel disappointed with yourself because you didn't have the courage to say what was really on your mind?
- Do you find yourself in conversations where multiple participants are advocating for their point of view without really listening to what others are saying?
- Do you ever find yourself thinking one way and acting another?

47

Chapter 5: Maintain Integrity

If you answered yes to any of these questions, then there is an opportunity to improve the integrity of your conversations.

Muster the courage

Some of the most important conversations we have require us to find the courage to get the tough stuff across the threshold of our lips and into the conversation. The higher the stakes of the conversation, the more this is true. We are most vulnerable when the stakes are high and there is a fear of divulging more than we should or offending someone else. In these conditions, we struggle speaking the tough stuff into the conversation.

Most people dislike conflict and will do anything to avoid it. As a result, they may keep real opinions to themselves. We don't want to get in trouble. We think that if we just comply and keep our mouth shut, we can avoid discomfort. This might work for a while, but it doesn't work when people are counting on you as a leader or a key member of the team. Sometimes, we don't speak up because we don't want to hurt other people's feelings. Most of the time, that would be a lie. The truth is that we get afraid. What gets in our way is all about ourselves.

- We don't want to suffer embarrassment
- We don't want to lose face
- We don't want to be wrong
- We don't want others to think less of us
- We don't want it discovered that we don't know

- We want to look good and avoid looking bad

To keep these fears from bringing our velocity to a screeching halt, we need to have the courage to come out from behind our self and tackle fear head-on. Courage is not the absence of fear. Courage is the willingness to act despite your fear.

Balance explaining and asking

For productive conversations, strike an appropriate balance between explaining your point of view and asking others for their opinion.

<u>Explaining or advocating</u> is expressing an idea or opinion and when done well it:

- helps others see what you see and how you think about an issue
- gives examples of the data you select and states the meaning you assign to the data
- explains the steps in your thinking
- identifies consequences without casting blame
- discloses your emotions without assuming the other is responsible for creating them.

<u>Asking or inquiring</u> is asking or exploring others thought and when done well it:

- Exposes how others see a situation to determine what you may be missing
- Seeks different viewpoints
- Asks others to give examples of the data they select and the meaning they assign to the data

Chapter 5: Maintain Integrity

- Asks others to explain the steps in their thinking
- When appropriate, asks others to explain what leads them to act as they do
- Asks about others' emotions
- Encourages others to identify gaps in your thinking
- Asks for help in seeing if you're unknowingly contributing to the problem

Not maintaining an appropriate balance of advocacy and inquiry can cause you to be out of integrity in the conversation and not get your desired results.

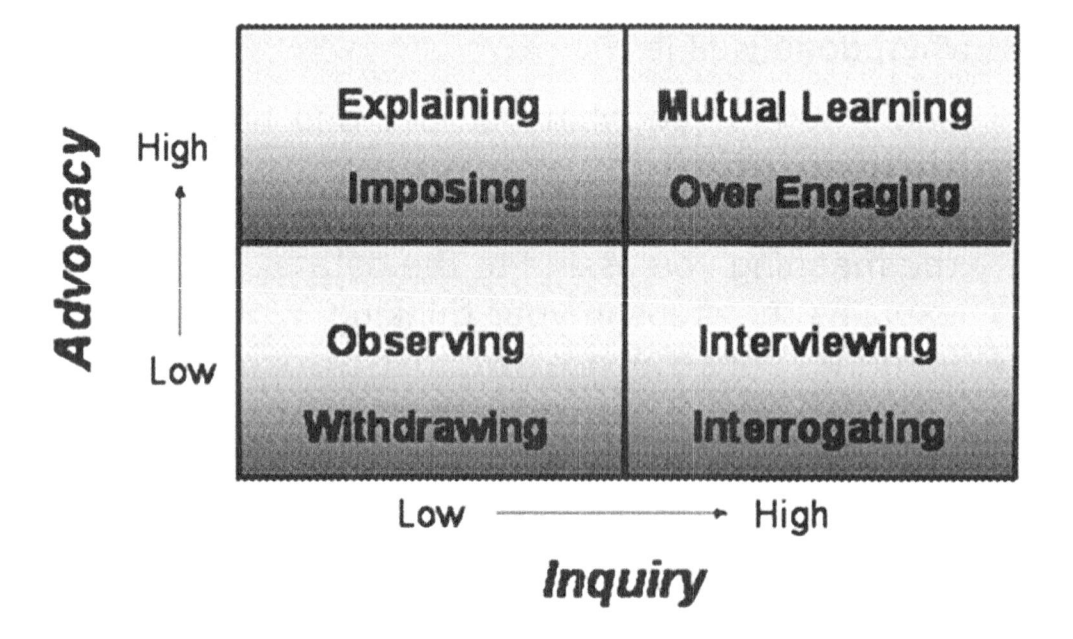

	Low Inquiry	**High Inquiry**
High Advocacy	Explaining / Imposing	Mutual Learning / Over Engaging
Low Advocacy	Observing / Withdrawing	Interviewing / Interrogating

Consider the chart above. When there is too much **advocating** going on, you impose or over-engage. When doing it with the right balance, you explain or engage in mutual learning.

However, if you're not **advocating** enough you show up as withdrawn or interrogating instead of being in balance and showing up as an observer or an interviewer.

When there is too much **inquiry**, you come off as over-engaging or interrogating. When doing it right, you appear engaged in mutual learning or interviewing. When there is too little **inquiry**, you come off as withdrawn or imposing. However, if you have the right balance, you come off as observing or explaining. The trick is maintaining a proper balance.

Balancing Advocacy and Inquiry	Examples of What to Say
Test your understanding of what others said	What I'm hearing you say (feel, think, react to, etc.) … Did I get that right? Have I missed anything?
Summarize	Here are the key points I heard…
State your views	The way I see it is … My concern is… Of the three options, I endorse…
Give examples that illustrate	Last year we were 30% under plan… When you said, 'Our morale is low,'… When you roll your eyes and sigh…

Chapter 5: Maintain Integrity

Balancing Advocacy and Inquiry (Continued)	Examples of What to Say (Continued)
Make your reasoning explicit	Competitor X just announced a new product that leap-frogs our own. It will take 2-years to do the same given our most recent setback.
State your conclusions as discussable options	One possibility is to look for a technology acquisition to regain our market advantage quickly. What path do to you favor?
Disclose your emotions, without assuming others are responsible for creating them	I'm feeling (concerned, upset, angry, frustrated...) by this conversation. Can we take a minute to talk about why?
Ask others for examples that illustrate their views	What are you seeing or hearing on this topic?
Ask others for the reasoning that connects their examples to their conclusions	Tell me more about how your example supports your conclusion. What assumptions are you making about why our technology is lagging?
Ask others for conclusions that flow from their reasoning	Given what you are saying, what do you think we ought to do to address our technology gap?
Seek a range of perspectives	John and I weighed in on this issue. What do the rest of you favor as options?

Chapter 5: Maintain Integrity

Balancing Advocacy and Inquiry (Continued)	Examples of What to Say (Continued)
Share the reason for your questions	I'm asking because you may see things from a sales perspective that I may have missed. I'm asking because between all of us, there is a lot of knowledge and different viewpoints in the room.
Encourage others to challenge your assumptions and conclusions	In what ways do you see the situation differently?" Can you draw a different conclusion? What am I missing?
Ask if you're unknowingly contributing to difficulties	Is there anything I am doing that is keeping us from finding a solution?

Chapter 5: Maintain Integrity

Poor (closed) Inquiry Questions	Great (open) Inquiry Questions
Don't you agree?	In what ways is your proposal different?
Do others feel that way too?	What concerns have others expressed to you on this proposal?
Do you understand what I'm trying to say?	What's your reaction to this proposal?
Did you do that because of this, that, or because of something else?	What leads you to that conclusion?
Why don't you just do what I'm suggesting?	What about my proposal concerns you?
Why didn't you just tell me?	What got in the way of you just telling me? Did I do or say something to make it difficult?

Dealing with Disagreement	Example of What to Say
Seek to understand others' views	I'm hearing you to say … What might I be missing?
Ask others to make their reasoning, concerns, and/or interests known	What concerns do you want to address? What are you considering from your perspective that I might not have considered?
State your reasoning, concerns, interests with the intention of learning if others can see gaps	Here's how I'm see it… What might I be missing?
Discover ways to address mutual concerns and interests	I'm concerned about… How would you approach addressing these concerns?

Chapter 5: Maintain Integrity

Getting Through an Impasse	Examples of What to Say
Acknowledge the impasse without blame	We seem to be stuck. Neither of us seems to be persuaded by the other. Is there another point of view we can examine the issue from?
Identify assumptions and beliefs that contribute to the impasse, and test how others see it. Ask others to help, if needed	We appear to be working from different assumptions. For example, … How are you seeing it differently? What assumptions are we making? How would another stakeholder view this?
Reflect on what would need to be different for you to change your perception of the issue	Conditions that would lead me to change my perception would be… Are you aware of any examples? What conditions, if present, would lead you to change your perception?
Test your assumption via experimentation	Let's gather data on… and use it to test our assumptions. Are you open to an experiment where we try both options for a brief period and then re-evaluate?
Get outside opinion. Identify a mutually trusted individual to help you reflect on your current thinking, and to invent alternatives	Who could we ask to help us examine our thinking, and come up with alternatives?

Be consistent in thoughts and actions

When you maintain consistency in thoughts and actions, you maintain integrity. When we think one way, yet act and speak in another way we are not acting in integrity. Integrity means telling the truth even if the truth is unpleasant. It is better to be honest than to delude others, because the reality is you delude yourself, too. When we listen to our hearts and do and say the right thing, life becomes far less complicated and more genuine.

Acting in integrity is a key element of conversations for results. We will speak more on integrity in conversations for action when we deal with accountability.

Chapter 6: Close the Loop

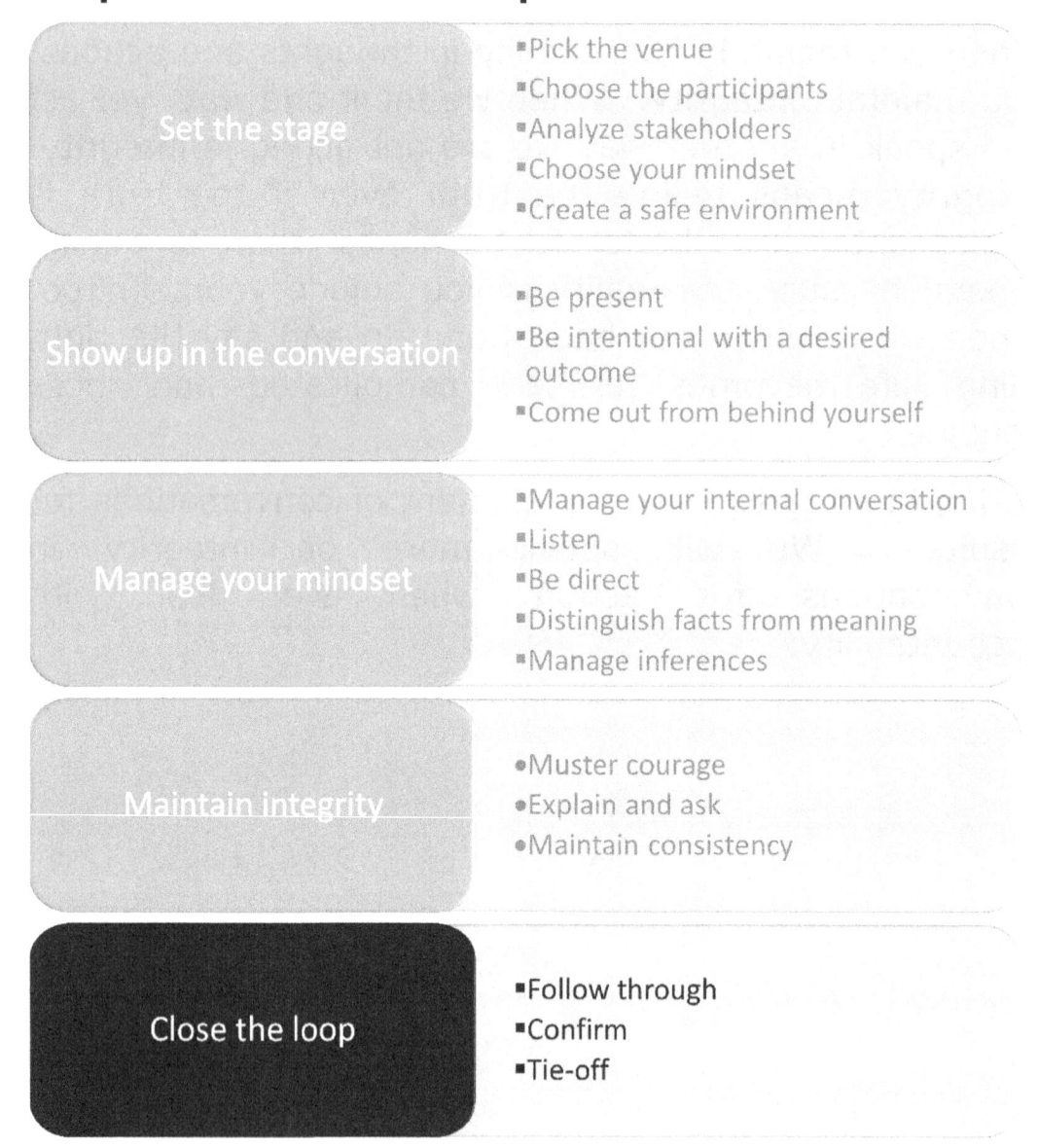

Set the stage
- Pick the venue
- Choose the participants
- Analyze stakeholders
- Choose your mindset
- Create a safe environment

Show up in the conversation
- Be present
- Be intentional with a desired outcome
- Come out from behind yourself

Manage your mindset
- Manage your internal conversation
- Listen
- Be direct
- Distinguish facts from meaning
- Manage inferences

Maintain integrity
- Muster courage
- Explain and ask
- Maintain consistency

Close the loop
- Follow through
- Confirm
- Tie-off

- Do you feel frustrated by people who do not follow up when they say they will?
- Do you feel a lack of clarity and closure after talking to some individuals?

- Do you ever notice groups come to an agreement, only to have it spin-off onto new topics without first gaining closure?

If you answered yes to any of these questions, then you have opportunities to improve **closing the loop**.

Follow Through

Some organizations experience a culture of complacency and a lack of follow through. This condition is a killer of productivity and performance. Raising the performance bar, working with a sense of urgency, following through quickly, and establishing a culture of accountability are great cures for a culture of complacency. It starts with keeping a list of commitments made to you and by you and diligently following up on them. When you set an expectation of follow-through in the initial conversation, the probability of it happening goes up dramatically. In your list, specify who initiates the follow through, by when, under what constraints, and with what deliverables.

Confirm

The follow-through is not complete until the person making the request confirms that the person with the action item meets the Conditions of Satisfaction. Without confirmation, the task remains in an open-loop state.

Chapter 6: Close the Loop

Tie-Off

The tie-off process is a terrific way to lock progress in when a group reaches a consensus. The technique is especially helpful when a goal requires a series of successive steps for completion. The technique is analogous to climbing a mountain. You climb to a point where you want to place an anchor. If you should fall, then you will not fall past the safety of the anchor. A good facilitator will identify these anchor points in advance and strive for consensus.

Consensus doesn't necessarily mean that everyone is in <u>total</u> agreement. It is only necessary for each participant to be in <u>basic</u> agreement. This means that if most of the group agrees, then those with basic agreement may consent to the group's decision.

However, if someone is uneasy with where the group is heading, it is necessary to surface and discuss their concern before moving forward. This is when some of the greatest insights emerge.

These are the guidelines for confirming buy-in before a Tie-Off.

- Everyone who has something to say has spoken
- Everyone can live with the decision of the group
- The group is taking a decision and not going back on it

We acknowledge tie-off with eye contact, then verbally and with a physical gesture. In the simplest form, the facilitator or leader looks directly at each person to get their vote by thumb. If there are thumbs down, find out why because you're not at a tie-off point. If some thumbs are at 10 or 11 o'clock, also find out why as there may be something useful to discover. Alternatively, the 10 or 11 o'clock individuals can indicate they are good with the decision if the rest of the group agrees strongly.

Agree, this is good

Basically agree, but with some hesitation and can go with the decision

Not there yet, something is off

Do not agree, this is wrong

When appropriate make a declaration, the group is at a tie-off point. A best practice has the group all stand and then, on the count of three, clap in unison. The action initially can feel awkward. Just do it and get over it! It publicly declares that the group is taking a decision and everyone is on board. When you stand and clap, there is no faking it. An individual may not later say they really didn't agree. The time to disagree is before the tie-off. When you participate, by definition, you agree with the decision. If you have worked with the author in the past or with the Center for Quality of Management, you may know this technique as a Yo-One. The only real difference is that the group yells "yo-one" in unison as they clap. Yo-one derives from other Japanese methods for marking group consensus and decisions.

However accomplished, once adopted as a meeting norm, it is amazing how quickly tying-off catches on and how powerfully it moves meetings to successful conclusions.

Part 2

Chapter 7: Types of Conversations

There are three broad categories of Conversations for Results.

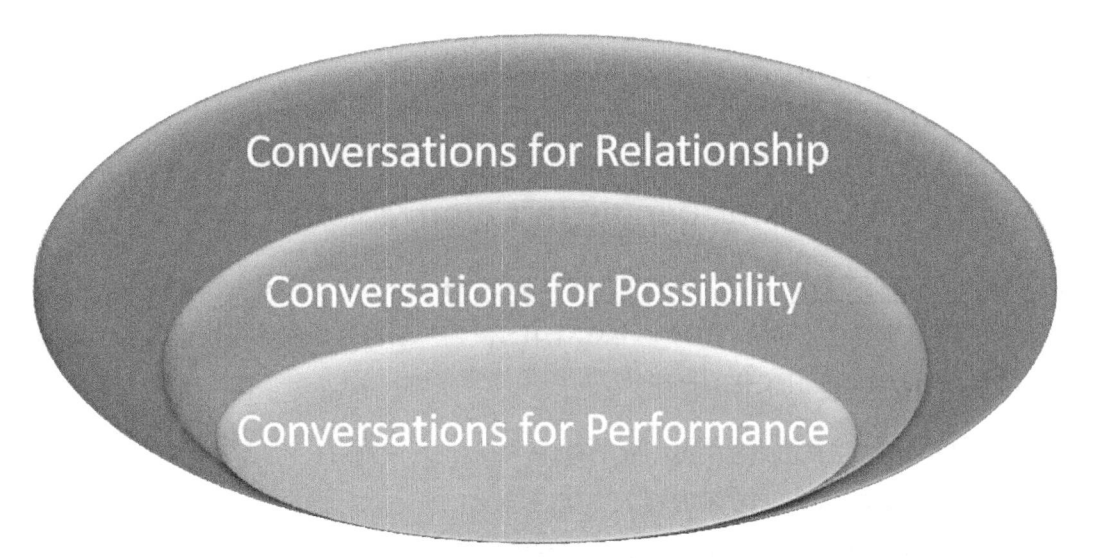

- Conversations for Relationship
- Conversations for Possibility
- Conversations for Performance

A typical progression starts with a Conversation for Relationship, which leads to Conversations for Possibility, which in turn lead to Conversations for Performance. The starting point and foundation are **Conversations for Relationship**. These conversations are about:

- building rapport by discovering things about the other individual
- relating to others' experiences
- checking for agreement or lack of alignment

Chapter 7: Types of Conversations

Once you've established a relationship, even if it's not a strong one, the second step is conducting **Conversations for Possibility**. These conversations facilitate:

- generating ideas and possibilities
- prioritizing multiple possibilities
- selecting possibilities
- enrolling other people into your ideas

Conversations for Performance are a powerful subset of Conversations for Results. **Conversations for Performance** include:

- Conversations for Action
- Conversations for Delegation
- Conversations for Accountability
- Conversations for Confrontation
- Conversations for Selling

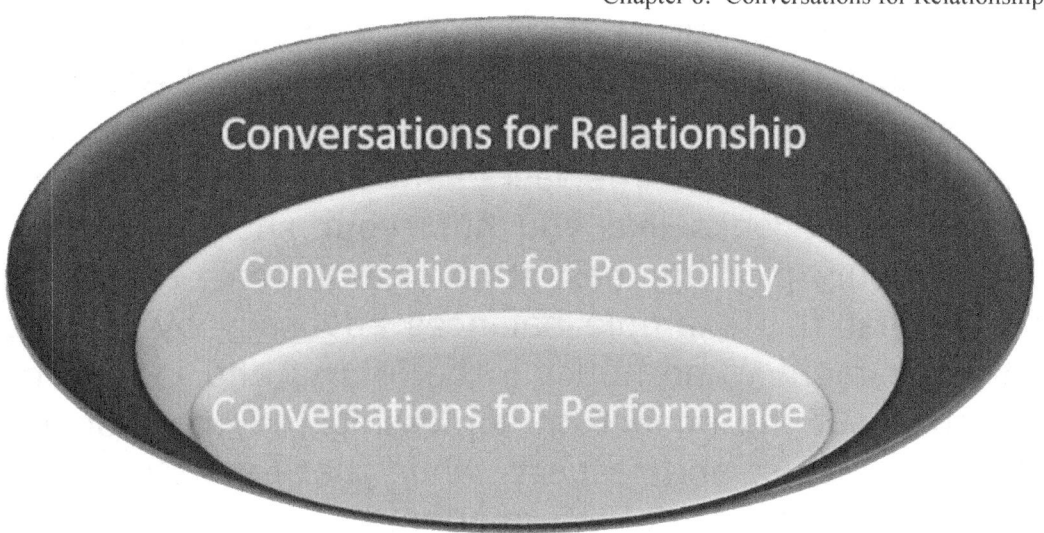

Chapter 8: Conversations for Relationship

Conversations for Relationship serve as a foundation for all other conversations. They allow you to connect with other people, and when those connections happen at a deep, authentic level, they accelerate the velocity of conversations to follow.

Rapport

Conversations for Relationship require building **Rapport**. That means spending time in the "we" space where there is common ground between you and others in the conversation. Sometimes we refer to this part of the conversation as small-talk. It's important for several reasons. Exploring the "we" space serves to create some common ground and acts as a leveling function between the participants. It serves to acknowledge and validate others and their experience.

Some people substitute **Report** for **Rapport** by stating facts about their lives without drawing in and engaging the other person. **Report** might sound like "The Trail Blazers won in overtime last night". **Rapport** sounds more like "It looks like you hurt your shoulder, will it affect your pick-up basketball game on Tuesday?" Notice that this example balances advocacy by making an assessment when noticing the injury, and inquiry by asking about the impact on something they care about. This builds trust and respect, while the Report example simply states a piece of information.

Keep in mind that the language of **Report** is about what is going on in the world. The language of **Rapport** is about what is going on in their world. As the well-known truism goes, "People don't care how much you know, until they know how much you care".

The African Zulu greeting "sawubona" demonstrates this well and serves as an example and an inspiration. It's a greeting that means more than hello. It means, "I see you". It means "I see your personality. I see your humanity. I see your dignity and I see your respect." The traditional response someone gives to, "sawubona" (I see you) is "ngikhona," which means, "I am here". The response is a little more complex than that. It tells the other person that you feel seen and understood, and that you appreciate the recognition of your personal dignity. Greeting people with this level of intention raises the bar way beyond "hello" and an insincere "how are you doing?" Imagine how wonderful it would feel when greeted by someone who really sees you and expresses they care. Imagine the impact you will have on the people you interact with if you hold the intention of seeing their individuality, their humanity, and their dignity, while demonstrating your respect.

It is necessary to be authentic. In a heartbeat, people can spot someone who is phony or trying too hard. They notice fake smiles and self-serving agendas. When we meet people for the first time, they judge us and form an opinion in the first few seconds of meeting. It is possible to accelerate the time it takes to make a positive impression by being natural and authentic.

An initial, instinctive reaction when meeting someone is determining if they are friendly or a threat. This feeds the fight, flight, or freeze response. I'm sure you've met people who trigger your flight response. Your initial reaction is thinking of how quickly you can end the interaction and move away. It's possible that they may be triggering an old memory of a terrible experience, or someone you dislike or distrust.

When you meet people for the first time they may judge you unfairly as well, due to no real fault of your own. To prevent this, quickly establish trust and allow people to connect with your human side more than your professional side. The human side is easier to trust and is where others feel safest.

Choosing your Attitude is a big part of sending the right signal in first interactions. More than anything else, your attitude determines your success or failure in

Conversations for Relationship. It's the attitude you choose that attracts people or has them fleeing as quickly as possible.

Many people respond as if their attitude is something caused by the events of their life. If things are not going well, their attitude might be poor, then the poor attitude repels others and causes more things to go bad. It becomes a vicious cycle: the events of their life affect their attitude; their attitude gets a poor response from others; and this brings on more negative events in their life.

Attitudes that repel include: arrogance, resentment, impatience, and hostility. If you've ever met someone with one of these attitudes you already know how unpleasant they are to be around.

In contrast, there are attitudes which build trust. These include: welcoming, empathy, resourcefulness, and curiosity. When you take on one of these attitudes your body language responds accordingly, people notice these cues and you get decidedly better outcomes.

Body language awareness isn't a skill we all have, but it is a skill you <u>can</u> learn. When you want to connect with someone look them in the eye and smile with your whole face. A good technique for making eye contact is noticing their eye color. A smile that doesn't reach your eyes doesn't appear genuine and heartfelt. Therefore, you need to use your whole face and have the smile engage your eyes, cheeks, and mouth. Once you've

Chapter 8: Conversations for Relationship

both made eye contact, break the eye bond; holding it too long can be disconcerting.

Another technique is **Opening Yourself** to the other person. Face them directly, with your body open and your hands visible. This signals you're friendly and not a threat. It is also helpful to match their body language and pace of speech. If they're expressive, you're expressive. If they're relaxed, you're relaxed. However, if they're highly agitated, don't match this tone as it can easily go bad.

When people like and trust you, they tend to see the best in you. When they don't like you or trust you, they tend to see the worst in you.

To connect in a meaningful way, get the other person to talk while you listen. It is an investment of your time that can pay off later in the form of trust when you need to get things done. Closed-ended questions typically get a one-word response like "yes" or "no" and don't keep the conversation going. Open-ended questions are effective at getting the ball rolling and often begin with the 5 "W's" and an "H": who, what, when, where, why, or how. To keep it from feeling like an interrogation, start with a brief statement, and follow with the open-ended question. For example, "You look sad. What's going on?" works far better than "Are you OK?".

To keep the conversation rolling, highlight something you heard that captured your interest and follow with a statement like, "tell me more". For example, "I am so sorry to hear about the loss of your Grand Mother. What is a favorite memory of her?". As the conversation gets rolling the other person will be looking for feedback. Both nonverbal and short verbal acknowledgments can work well to provide clues that you're really listening.

Trust

The foundation for solid relationships is **Trust**. Trust as a concept covers a lot of territory. To understand and improve **Trust**, let's consider it in terms of foundational elements. If you wrote trust as an equation, it would be:

$$Trust = f \frac{(Credibility) \times (Empathy)}{(Risk)}$$

Notice that **Risk** resides in the denominator of the equation. If there is little at **Risk** then the other elements are not so critical. As **Risk** goes up in a relationship **Trust** becomes super relevant. Notice also that the numerator consists of two elements; **Credibility** and **Empathy**. Because of the multiplicative relationship between **Credibility** and **Empathy**, if either goes to zero, then trust goes to zero.

To better understand trust, let's further break down the elements of credibility and empathy into subcomponents.

Credibility consists of competence, consistency, and courage. If an individual does not have the skills or training to be competent at a task, then the ability to trust them to successfully complete that task becomes low. On the flipside, if someone has the skills, experience, and training to complete a routine task, then it's reasonable to trust their competence in completing the task. **Competence** addresses the question of whether someone can complete an assignment.

Someone may be competent at completing tasks, but if they are inconsistent in their delivery, then trust becomes an issue. Consistency primarily takes the form of the quality of their work, the timeliness of their delivery, or their attitude. **Consistency** addresses the question of whether someone will reliably complete the assignment.

The third element of credibility is courage. When we say courage in this context, we mean, "do they have the courage to try innovative ideas and to do the right thing even if it's not popular?" If you question an individual's integrity to step-up and act courageously, especially when the stakes are high, then trust becomes an issue.

Empathy consists of caring, compassion and character. If an individual does not have your best interests at heart, then trust is going to be an issue. Likewise, if you want to have a positive relationship with someone, then empathy needs to come through as part of your conversations. To demonstrate empathy, it's necessary to let people know you care. One way to demonstrate caring is by asking about the people and things the other person holds dear. This may be their family, their hobbies, their work, or their health. Obviously, you need to treat what they care about with respect. Making fun of something they hold dear is a certain way to damage trust.

Compassion at work involves being considerate of the degree the other person is at risk or hurting. Expressing compassion involves being soft on the individual, even though you may need to be tough on the issue or their behavior.

A major component of **Character** as it relates to trust is the ability to keep a confidence. It also entails living your values and being truthful. For people to open-up in conversation, they need to know they are safe when sharing a vulnerability. They need to feel you're going to respect their disclosure and not cause them any future harm.

Asking the other person to complete a **Trust Wheel Assessment** when trust is lacking in a critical relationship can be a productive way to improve trust. The Trust Wheel consists of a spider diagram with a 1 through 5 rating scale. The traits on the right side correspond to credibility and include: competence, consistency, courage. The traits on the left side correspond to empathy and include: caring, compassion and character.

Chapter 8: Conversations for Relationship

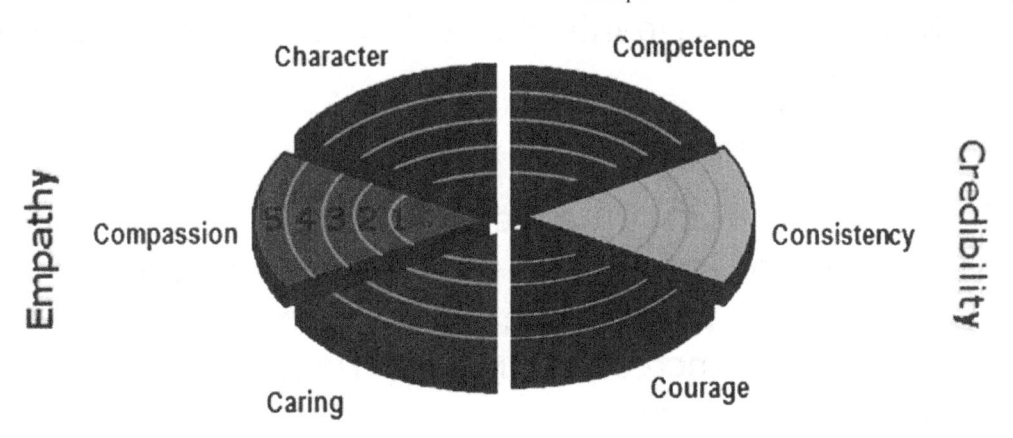

Trust Wheel diagram with labels: Character, Competence, Compassion, Consistency, Caring, Courage, Empathy, Credibility

Each person completes the trust wheel evaluation by answering the question from the point of view of "How do I think the other person would rate me on each item?" Once complete, one at a time, individuals share the evaluation and why they gave the rating. The other party confirms what they hear. The other party may agree, saying, "actually I would rate you higher" or "here's why I would rate you lower". By anticipating the other persons rating, it takes some of the judgmental sting from the conversation. It makes what may have been otherwise undiscussable, discussable and the focal point of a productive conversation. This often leads to a breakthrough in the relationship. Without communication skills and a reasonable amount of emotional intelligence, the conversation can go very poorly quickly. If the situation is very tense, consider using a facilitator to assist with the conversation. A skilled facilitator will establish and enforce ground rules. They will also insist the conversation happens directly

73

between the participants and will keep from being drug into the middle.

Trust and Intimacy

The level of trust in a relationship affects the level intimacy in conversations. You do not need trust in a relationship to speak in the language of report. As the level of trust increases in the relationship, rapport becomes easier to create.

Intimacy in Conversation Continuum

Low — Report ————————————— Rapport — High

Level of Trust ———————— TMI

The concept of "too much information" or "TMI" kicks in when the information shared exceeds the level of established rapport. For example, it is OK to ask anyone "how about those (insert favorite sport team name)?" However, if you have not established an elevated level of trust and rapport, it would be inappropriate to ask, "how are you dealing with the loss after your testicular cancer?" The biggest risk occurs when the other individual does not believe that you have their best interest at heart, or when they do not believe you will keep a confidence.

Some people are trust givers and open quickly, while other people are trust earners and require you to establish trust before advancing in the relationship.

Here are ways to increase trust and the level of intimacy in your conversations:

Chapter 8: Conversations for Relationship

To Increase Trust	What it looks Like	Ways to Kill Trust
Seek first to understand	Listen to others before advocating for your position.	Focusing only on getting your point of view across.
Offer trust	Be the first to extend trust, within reasonable boundaries based on the situation.	Remaining closed and untrusting. Micro managing employees.
Straight talk	Speak the truth in love and caring. Tell it like it is, while respecting the individual.	Withholding information, putting too much spin on the message.
Face reality	Confront the tough issues head-on. Muster the courage to get difficult messages across the threshold of your lips.	Ignoring "the elephant in the room" and operating in a space of denial.
Show respect	Offer respect for everyone. Recognize and preserve the dignity of all others regardless of their station in life.	Acting rude toward others, especially those who are dependent on you in some way. Showing a lack of concern for others. Being dismissive, diminishing, or belittling.

To Increase Trust (Continued)	What it looks Like	Ways to Kill Trust
Admit and correct mistakes	Apologize when wrong, commit to restoring any losses and ensure the offense will not happen again.	Trying to hide mistakes or passing the blame when you're wrong. Ignoring the situation.
Demonstrate improvement	When you let someone down, be sure they see your efforts to improve.	Continue making the same offenses. Try to pass off activity for results.
Operate transparently	Be open, honest, genuine, and verifiable.	Operating with hidden agendas. Creating appearances different from reality.
Demonstrate loyalty	Maintain the integrity of information shared in confidence.	Disclosing confidential information. Throwing others under the bus. Talking bad behind others back.
	Cover someone's back as in "I've got your 6"	
Deliver results	Deliver on-time, every time, with high quality.	Missing deadlines and not following through on promises.

Building Rapport

The following assessment offers ways to self-evaluate your skills in building rapport during your **Conversations for Relationship**. There are a lot of items that need skillful execution.

Chapter 8: Conversations for Relationship

Rapport Building Assessment

When sitting, did you lean slightly forward, towards the person you're talking to, with hands open and arms and legs uncrossed?	Yes☐ Partial☐ No☐ N/A☐
Did you look at the other person about ½ of the time making eye-contact?	Yes☐ Partial☐ No☐ N/A☐
Were you careful not to make them feel uncomfortable with too much eye contact?	Yes☐ Partial☐ No☐ N/A☐
When listening, did you give nods, and make encouraging sounds affirming your interest?	Yes☐ Partial☐ No☐ N/A☐
Did you remember to smile using your whole face?	Yes☐ Partial☐ No☐ N/A☐
Did you use the other person's name early in the conversation to be polite and reinforce the name in your mind?	Yes☐ Partial☐ No☐ N/A☐
Did you ask open-ended questions?	Yes☐ Partial☐ No☐ N/A☐
Did you summarize, reflect, and clarify back to the other person what you think they have said, thereby giving the opportunity to clear any misunderstandings quickly?	Yes☐ Partial☐ No☐ N/A☐
Did you talk about things that refer to what the other person previously said and find links between common experiences?	Yes☐ Partial☐ No☐ N/A☐
Did you show empathy by demonstrating that you understand how the other person feels and can see things from their point of view?	Yes☐ Partial☐ No☐ N/A☐
When in agreement with the other person, did you openly say so and say why?	Yes☐ Partial☐ No☐ N/A☐
Did you build on the other person's ideas without hijacking the conversation?	Yes☐ Partial☒ No☐ N/A☐
Were you non-judgmental towards the other person, letting go of stereotypes and any preconceived ideas you may have about the person?	Yes☐ Partial☐ No☐ N/A☐
Did you admit when you don't know the answer or made a mistake?	Yes☐ Partial☐ No☐ N/A☐
Were you genuine, with visual and verbal behaviors working together to maximize the impact of your communication?	Yes☐ Partial☐ No☐ N/A☐
Did you offer a compliment, avoid criticism and be polite?	Yes☐ Partial☐ No☐ N/A☐
Did you ask for a small piece of advice that highlights a skillset of the other person?	Yes☐ Partial☐ No☐ N/A☐

If you find there are multiple areas to improve, try tackling one or two at a time. More than that can become overwhelming. Before long you will be able to assess yourself with a long string of yes check marks.

Group Rapport Building

When working with individuals or groups, try running a "check-in" prior to getting down to business. This can be an effective practice for building rapport or moving a group forward. The purposes of the "check-in" are:

- Allowing people to become present in the meeting by dumping concerns that may or may not be relevant to the meeting.
- Building rapport by disclosing more about ourselves and learning more about others.
- Letting others know we care by offering a safe way to share news and concerns.

It is helpful to have a theme for the check-in so people have a focus for their sharing. In an emotion-based check-in, participants share one thing that currently makes them either mad, glad, sad, delighted, excited, or concerned.

Design the check-in question to match the event. Some factors to consider include:

- How much time do you have for the check-in? Think about how big your question is – does it invite a three to five-minute story from each person, or a sentence or two?

- How can the check-in connect and support the rest of the agenda and the overall purpose of the gathering?
- What kind of tone do you want to create through the check-in? Playful? Serious? Connecting? Learning something new about each other?
- Is this a group familiar with check-ins and have been meeting together regularly? Maybe, it's time to mix things up with some fun.

A check-in question such as, "Tell us the story of how you originally came into this work," will open the story space and would be a longer check-in process. A check-in question like, "Say a few words on what it was like getting here today" or, "Is there anything on your mind that you want to share so you can be present today" could be a shorter check-in.

For a type-A personality, check-ins may be frustrating and appear as a waste of time. Consider that sometimes you must go slower in the beginning to go faster and farther. Often, it's not about sending one person ahead of the group to plant a flag on top of a summit, it's about getting the entire group to the summit. If you need to go fast, then go alone. If you need to go far, then go in a group. Are you running a sprint or a marathon?

Discovery

Approach conversations with a mindset of discovery. Listen for what is new, how it may help you see situations and other's point of view more clearly.

The discovery element of Conversations for Relationship is learning about the other person and their world. We touched on many of the techniques earlier when we covered building rapport.

The most powerful tool beyond an open mind, is asking **open ended questions**. This allows the other person to tell their story. "Why" questions help you understand their point of view. If asked multiple times in succession, "why" questions can quickly get you to the heart of an issue. To prevent "why" questions from feeling like an interrogation, it's helpful to sometimes ask in the form of "help me understand …"

If you come across like you are interrogating a suspect, where "anything said can and will be used against you," then you should not expect the other person to be at ease nor open. Treat the relationship discovery as an explorer seeking to discover something new and exciting.

Relating

The relating element of Conversations for Relationship is making a connection with the other person by discovering common interests where you both relate. When done well, relating has an element of empathy for another person's experience. You may find yourself saying "I can relate, as I had a similar experience…" Relating increases rapport in the relationship.

Agreement

When Conversations for Relationship go well, you may find yourself with common points of view where you agree. At other times, you may find you have opposing views with no agreement. Nonagreement is not the end of the world; it's an opportunity to ask open ended questions to discover how the other person came to hold their opinion. This creates a climate where learning and insight are most abundant. Be sure to value diversity with respect when there is nonagreement.

Communication in Groups

When working in groups, understanding the **Stage of Community** is key. This gives clues on what techniques to use to move the group forward. There are four stages:

1. **Pseudo-community** is how strangers show-up at a cocktail party at a museum. Most everyone appears pleasant, yet superficial.
2. **Chaos** is what it's like to get a group of "take control" strangers to come up with an idea of where to go. They spend a lot of time trying to lobby for their desired outcome. This becomes a frustrating process with little to no real progress.
3. **Emptying** is a necessary step to get to real community. During this level, individuals begin to speak authentically and others engage in active listening. Individuals suspend lobbying for their desired outcome and let go of the need to control in favor of trying to understand others.

4. In **Community**, individuals experience a safe place to share. They appreciate and celebrate interpersonal differences and allow others to "be themselves." Respect and acceptance become the norm and there is grace in dealing with disagreements. Individuals share equally and decide more effectively as they authentically communicate. High performance teams spend most of their time in Stage 4 of community.

This model for community isn't static; the process requires ongoing awareness and shared leadership effort to keep the conversations productive.

When working with groups, the level of community influences the group's ability to reach agreement.

Stage 1: Pseudo-community

What people do in this stage:	To move a group forward:
• Appear extremely pleasant & avoid all disagreements	• Surface differences you hear
• Maintain a pretense that denies individual differences	• Create ground rules that make it safe to increase the level of honesty
• Tell white lies, withhold truth and true feelings to avoid conflict	• Take a risk and share what you're experiencing
• Speak in vague generalities while focusing on superficial topics	• Challenge assumptions in a productive, supportive manner
	• Refuse to engage in a false sense that "everything's great"

Chapter 8: Conversations for Relationship

What people do in this stage:	*To move a group forward:*
Stage 2: Chaos	
• Engage in well intentioned attempts to heal and convert others • Don't pretend there are no differences; try to remove them • Try to "convert" others to the prevailing "norm" • Unproductive, circular conflict and struggle - uncomfortable for most	• Don't suppress the conflict/emotion • Focus people on the issues & behaviors and don't allow personal attacks • Reinforce honest, productive communication • Support the use of ground rules to keep the environment safe • Redirect declarations, assertions, and assumptions into questions
Stage 3: Emptying	
• Empty the barriers to authentic communication (our solutions only, prejudices, judgments) • Listen Actively • Stop trying to convert and change others • Let go of need to control	• Focus on being" with" people • Model active listening • Express your own emotions & observations • Verbally & non-verbally support people talking about "the hard stuff"

What people do in this stage:	To *move a group forward*:
Stage 4: Community	
• Experience a safe place to share • Appreciate & celebrate interpersonal differences • Allow themselves and others to "be themselves;" respect & acceptance is the norm • Fight gracefully, share equally, decide more effectively • Authentic communication is present & experienced	• Reflect to the group periodically how they're communicating & being • Encourage the group to "stay in" this space • Understand this process is cyclical and requires ongoing effort, even in a mature team and relationships

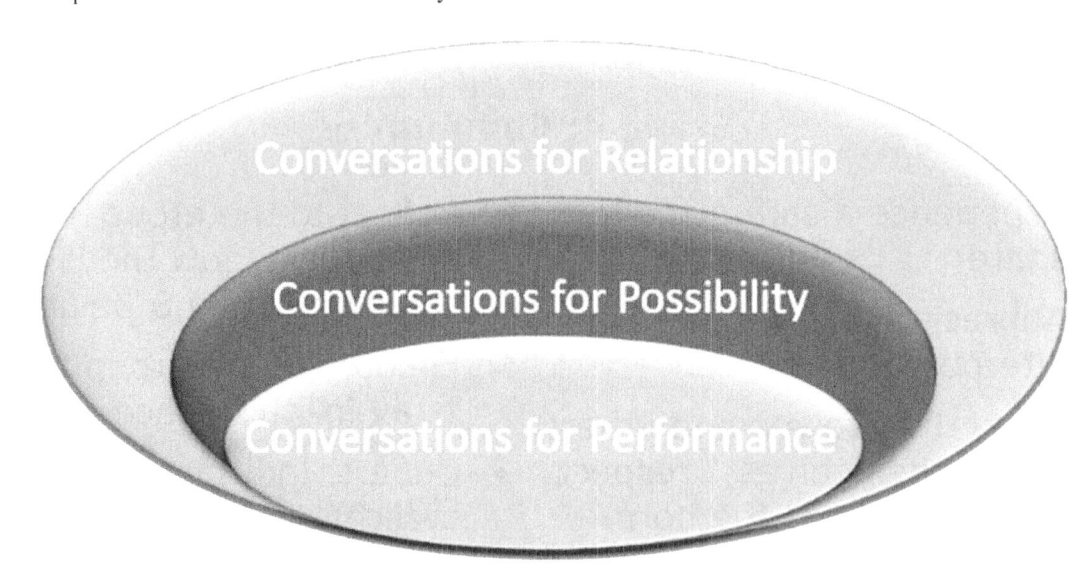

Chapter 9: Conversations for Possibility:

Once you've established a relationship, even if it's not a strong relationship, the second type of conversation in a typical sequence is **Conversations for Possibility**.

At an individual level, Conversations for Possibility can be as simple as "where do we go for lunch"? The idea is to explore what might be. When you are clear that you are exploring options and not taking a decision at this point, you open the space for more ideas to emerge. When you suspend decision making individuals are more at ease to offer interesting options.

Sometimes you are exploring what might be possible in a relationship. A job interview has a strong element of possibility even though you are not brainstorming. You may be exploring the possibility of continuing a relationship and defining what that might look like.

Innovation Across an Organization

At the organizational or group level, **Conversations for Possibility** conform nicely into an **Innovation Challenge**. An Innovation Challenge is a tournament designed to engage small teams or the entire organization with a focus on improving processes, finding new products or services, or addressing strategic initiatives. In realm of Innovation, teams that use Conversations for Possibility always create more powerful results than teams that lack this skill-set.

The Challenge can generate innovative ideas through: brainstorming ideas; prioritizing multiple possibilities; selecting possibilities; and enrolling team mates in viable solutions.

Ideation

Ideation is simply the process of generating ideas or brainstorming. When we have conversations for possibility, we start by coming up with what's possible. This could be anything from picking a location for an off-site meeting or deciding what features to include in a new product offering.

Creating well-defined parameters will make the **Ideation Process** more effective. "Let's have our next team meeting in Cabo," sounds great until you determine the budget for the meeting. Or that the parameters for this brainstorming session are "we need ways to engage with the age 20-25 market within the next month."

Chapter 9: Conversations for Possibility:

Ideation is at the heart of innovation. Innovation occurs when you consider two or more ideas or observations while also considering your target.

Bill Gordon's story is a great example. Bill had the task of minimizing breakage in potato chip bags while working at Proctor and Gamble. He found a "conceptual twin" for potato chips when raking leaves in his yard. On a dry sunny day, he noticed that leaves crumble when shoved into the bag. On a rainy day, wet leaves didn't break. In fact, each wet leaf conformed to the shape of its neighbor, making it easy to pack the bag. The idea of wetting and forming moist potato flour in a specific shape gave Pringles its start in 1968.

Bill thought about his problem while considering multiple ideas and observations. When you start generating ideas, you don't always initially know what has merit and what doesn't. It may not be a single idea that wins the day. Most often, it is a combination of ideas combined in a unique way.

Idea Generation is far more effective if performed in a group, rather than relying on the inspiration of a single individual.

Generating a lot of ideas quickly is a key practice in a successful Innovation Challenge. As the number of ideas increases, the quality of the best idea typically increases. Eventually, you'll hit a point of diminishing return, but that usually occurs after a hundred or more ideas get generated.

Chapter 9: Conversations for Possibility:

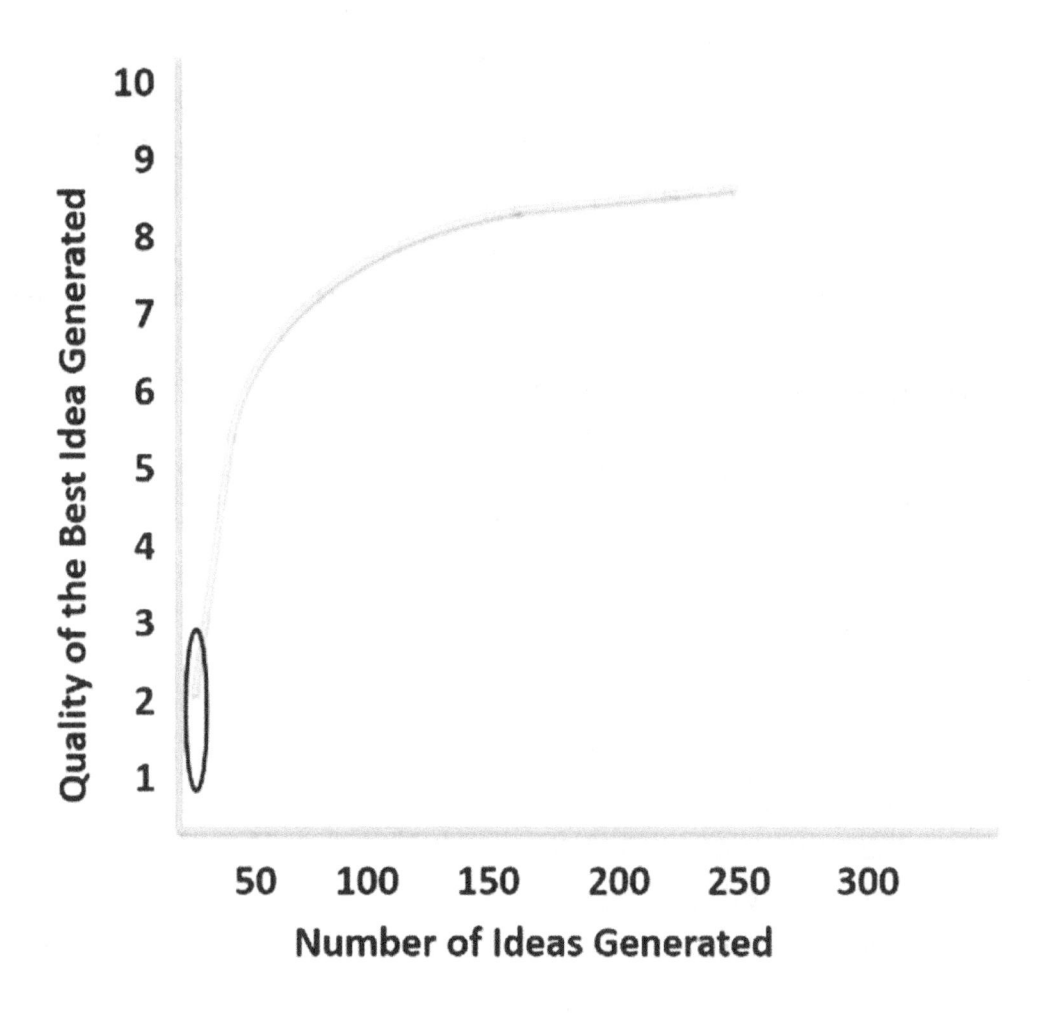

[Graph: Quality of the Best Idea Generated (y-axis, 1-10) vs. Number of Ideas Generated (x-axis, 50-300). Curve rises steeply then levels off around 8-9. An oval highlights the low range near the origin.]

How often are we thrilled to have six to 12 ideas to consider, when addressing a problem? By engaging in **Conversations for Possibility** effectively, you can increase the probability of a powerful breakthrough by an order of magnitude.

When ideating, look for diverse ideas. Variance is your friend. The faster you generate ideas, the higher the probability of a breakthrough.

Chapter 9: Conversations for Possibility:

Safe environments generate more possibilities, so you'll need to set ground rules prior to your brainstorming session. Consider allowing the team to create their own by performing a mini-brainstorming session around ground rules. This provides an opportunity to practice the necessary skills for a brainstorming session and it allows the team to take ownership of what is acceptable and unacceptable behavior.

Once the group generates a ground rules list, be sure to **Tie-Off** and post them in a highly visible location for the session.

Four key ground rules that are useful when conducting a brainstorming session:

1. There are no dumb ideas. Period. It is a brainstorming session, not a serious matter that requires only serious solutions. This is one of the fun activities; keep it that way.
2. Don't criticize other people's ideas. It is not a debate, discussion, or forum for one person to display superiority over another. You want to quickly generate many diverse ideas. The prioritization and scrubbing of the ideas happens later.
3. Build on other people's ideas. Often an idea suggested by one person can trigger a bigger and/or better idea by another person. Or a variation of an idea on the board could be the next "post-it note" idea. It is this building of ideas that

leads to out of the box thinking and innovative ideas.
4. Go for quantity over quality. We are looking to generate many diverse ideas and some will be wild and crazy while others may be close to perfect. We need them all at this stage. Here, we want quantity; the more creative the ideas, the better.

As a first pass after defining your target focus, generate ideas individually. This allows you to go fast without waiting for a group discussion. However, it is not just one person writing, but many writing simultaneously to quickly generate many ideas.

Once you have a core set of ideas, teams can talk about the ideas and combine them and make variations to come up with even better ideas. One effective technique for improving on ideas is the **SCAMMPER** method. It stands for:

- **S**ubstitute something
- **C**ombine it with something
- **A**dapt something to it
- **M**odify
- **M**agnify
- **P**ut to some other use
- **E**liminate or reduce something
- **R**everse or Rearrange it

Although individual ideas sometimes stand on their own merit, most solutions are the result of combining multiple ideas.

Chapter 9: Conversations for Possibility:

Prioritization

Once you have a pool of ideas, you need a way to prioritize them prior to selection/voting. Rank each based on the ease or cost of implementation, how well the idea addresses the target problem, and/or the potential impact or return when implemented. Consider using a wall chart to organize ideas.

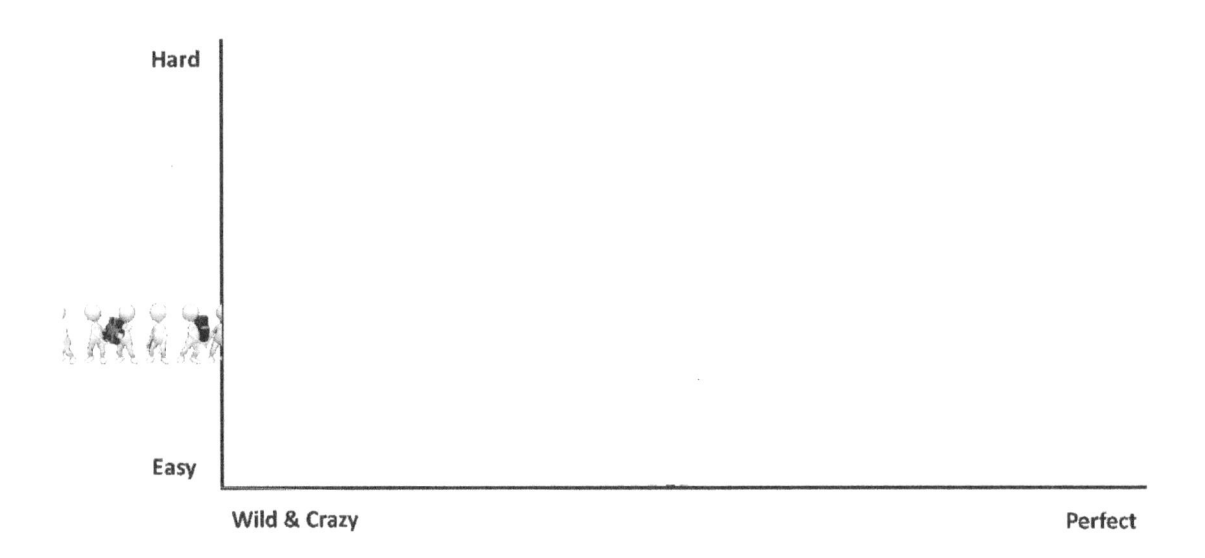

```
Hard |
     |
     |
     |
     |
     |
     |
     |
Easy |_____
     Wild & Crazy                  Perfect
```

The vertical axis (y-axis) represents effort to implement. The horizontal axis (x-axis) represents feasibility. Feasibility ranges from wild and crazy, to the threshold of something useful, to perfect. When rating and placing ideas on this chart, the most viable ideas show up in the lower right corner. This is where you find the ideas that are **Easy and Feasible.**

After an initial placement, get even more useful ideas by examining the posted ideas and asking what is their redeeming characteristic and how can you tweak the idea to improve its rating. Combine multiple ideas into an even better option.

The wall chart works well for smaller team meetings. When expanding an Innovation Tournament to organization-wide proportions, use a web-based Idea Management System (IMS) designed for the task.

Solution Selection

A solution is one or more ideas combined together that address the challenge target. You may select your solution from a single idea already generated. Or even better, take the additional step of combining ideas into complete solutions. Most innovation happens when multiple ideas combine. For example, a peanut butter cup is the combination of chocolate, peanut butter, and a cupcake muffin holder.

The team places solutions on a chart just as they did with the individual ideas.

Often, there are many Ideas or Solutions to evaluate on the first pass. On your first pass, screen them based on the underlying merit of the solution, not the quality of the submission. Simply separate the solutions with little to no merit from those that have a high potential.

Before voting, keep in mind the initial target of your brainstorming session. Then, use the dot voting method: place a dot on those **Ideas** or **Solutions** you want to promote. Base the voting on the idea's ability to address the target and meet any established criteria. There can be an unlimited number of votes (dots) applied, but only one dot per idea in this round. Other than seeking quick clarifications, avoid discussion during this phase; simply vote. When all voters have cast their votes, remove the ideas with no dots. This leave only those ideas that have "been voted in." This process repeats until you get down to 10 or 20 ideas. Optionally, group ideas in to similar clusters in-between voting rounds so it is easier to compare them. Eventually the voting method changes. Each participant then gets a set number of larger dots they can place on the ideas. This time the participants take turns placing their dots in sequence. They explain the reason for their vote as it gets cast. In this example, allow multiple large dots per idea or solution. This way, one or more clear winning ideas will emerge.

As an alternative, give each team member a set number of votes they can distribute however they choose. For example, each participant may receive a total of 10 votes to distribute. One idea may get multiple votes from the same person. After everyone votes, arrange the ideas in priority order based on the number of votes. Set aside those with no votes, first checking to ensure you are not throwing the baby out with the bath water. Repeat the process if necessary.

Revisit the project goals so you consider solutions based on their ability to address the underlying concern. That said, be open to by-chance-opportunities that pop-up which have high merit but may not be in alignment with the project. These can be forwarded to those who may be interested in a great idea related to their work. Allow teams with competing solutions to refine their presentation several times. This enables them to work out deficiencies and enable the best solution to emerge after several rounds of voting in the best solutions.

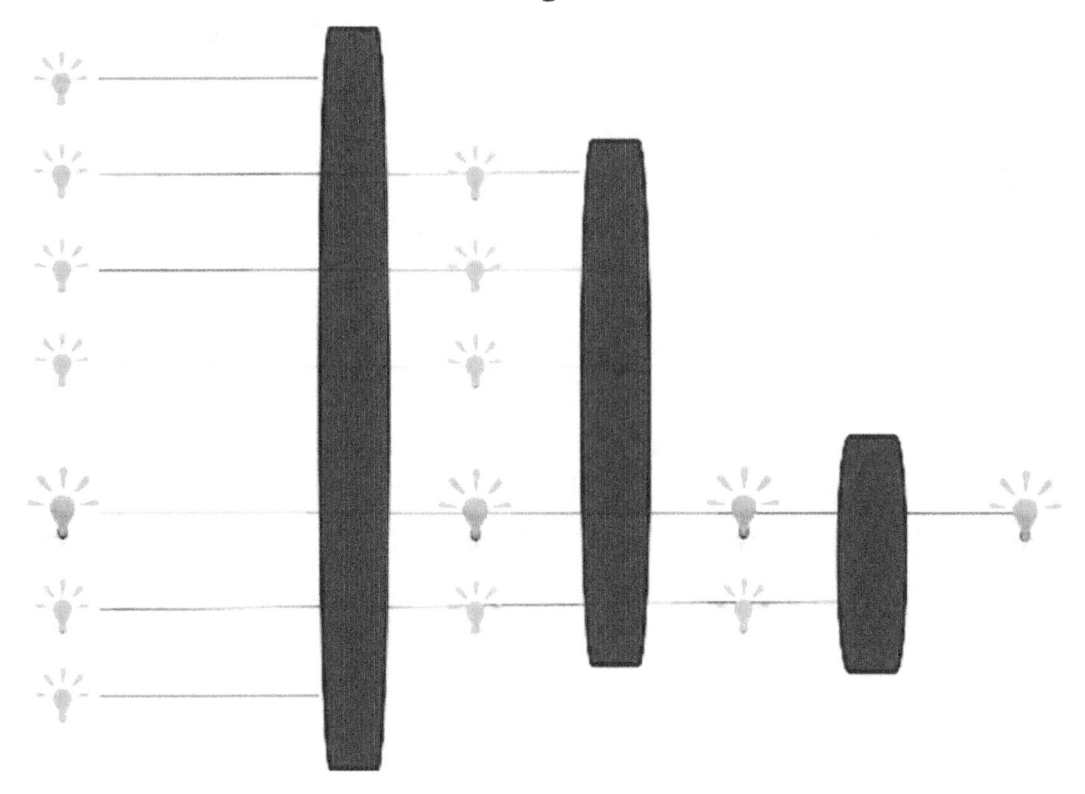

Enroll

Traditionally, "enroll" means to register as a member or to recruit someone to perform a service. For our purposes, "enroll" refers to persuading others to adopt a possibility or solution that you favor. Ideally, some excitement about the preferred possibility will start to show in the prioritization and selection stages.

Chapter 9: Conversations for Possibility:

Individually, we generate ideas that run through our own internal filters. This limits the diversity and sometimes the quality. When multiple individuals generate ideas together, the quantity and quality of the ideas tends to increase. More ideas emerge, so the possibility of a good one emerging goes up. This is due to differing points of view and the discussions that lead to new insights. Practice explaining your idea and your reasoning behind your endorsement and balancing that with asking others for their opinions and reasoning.

When you "sell" your preferred solution to the stakeholders, don't rely on your own charm. Package the idea in a way that gives it more charisma and appeal. Gain leverage for your personal power by letting the merit of the solution you champion do the heavy lifting. Be cautious about what solutions or causes you champion, as they can lift you up, or drag you under.

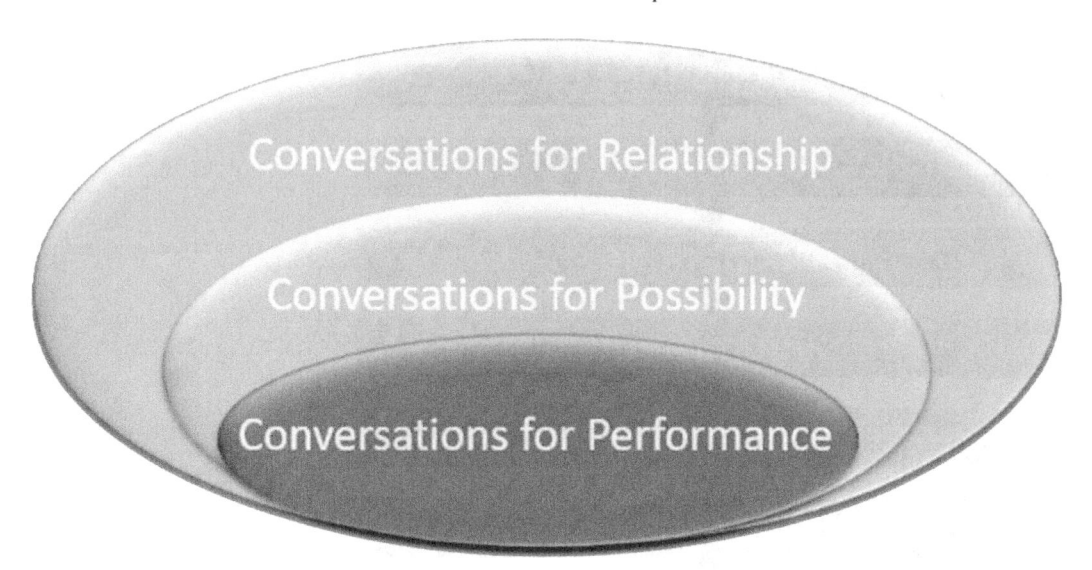

Chapter 10: Conversations for Performance:

Conversations for Performance is where work happens in an organization. They build upon **Conversations for Relationship** and usually, but not always, follow **Conversations for Possibility**.

There are several types of Conversations for Performance and the heart consists of Conversations for Action. Conversations for Action arise from a simple model. This model is extremely powerful in transforming organizations and in getting results.

The main activities in **Conversations for Performance** include:

Chapter 10: Conversations for Performance:

Preparing
↓
Requesting
↓
Negotiating
↓
Promising
↓
Performing
↓
Maintaining Accountability
↓
Diagnosing
↓
Improving

Building Blocks

We use language building blocks to construct powerful conversations that create the future we desire. The primary building blocks include:

- Declarations
- Assertions
- Promises
- Requests

Declarations

New ideas are expressed with **Declarations;** they are a powerful way to create something new via language. For example, consider the United States Declaratation of Independence. Commiting those words to print in the form of a declaration created a great nation. Another familiar declaration is "I now pronounce you husband and wife". Before the words are spoken, there is a relationship and possibilities, but no marriage. After the public Declaration, the spoken words, the union exists. When done well, declarations create clarity and alignment in organizations. They often create policy and set strategy.

Assertions

Assertions are confident statements of fact or belief. While **Declarations** create something new, **Assertions** state the way things are or are about to be. The distinction is in the act of creation. Here are some examples of assertions:

- The computer is on the table.
- It is going to rain.
- If you do not finish this work on 6:00 tonight, I will reassign the project to someone else.
- When you speak harshly, I cannot work productively with you because I feel annoyed.

A subtle but important aspect of an assertion is that the speaker stands behind the truth of the claim and takes the consequences if it is not true.

Promises

Making a **Promise** is special type of Declaration that binds us to action. We exchange them daily; managing **Promises** makes or breaks reputations. **Promises** are the foundation of **Conversations for Action** and the foundation of powerful organizations.

Promises beget trust. When we receive a promise, we extend hope that the individual will fulfill the promise. The cost of a broken promise is high as it damages both trust and reputation. Integrity is not about keeping all our promises all the time. It's about what we say and do, and how we act, when we break our promises.

Requests

Requests create actions that change the future. When you ask: "Will you marry me?" no matter the answer, you have created a future that would not have otherwise existed. Promises are often in response to a request. Requests initiate future action, and action is what makes things happen.

There are many types of conversations built using these building blocks. They include:

- Conversations for Action
- Conversations for Delegation
- Conversations for Accountability
- Conversations for Confrontation
- Conversations for Selling

Conversations for Action

Have you ever worked for the type of boss who doesn't delegate well? Sometimes they use the **Bring Me a Rock method**. This is where the boss asks you to bring them a rock without specifying the requirements. So, you dutifully go find any rock and bring it to them. Whereby, they proceed to tell you they want a different rock, it should be smooth. Being a good doer, you go find a smooth rock. When presented, you learn it's too small and should be blue in color. So, you search and find a smooth, not-too-small, blue rock, only to find your rock to be sub-par and that there are even more new requirements.

The **Bring Me a Rock game** plays out all too often in the corporate environment, simply because many managers are unwilling or unable to convey their needs and requirements in a way that allows their staff to create new products, processes, or proposals that are acceptable. There are several reasons this happens.

- Upper management is uncertain of its expectations and goals, and has not provided clarity for the manager. Stuck in the middle, the manager wants to minimize risk so they vie for time, waiting for clarity to come from above.
- The key decisionmaker is not good at making decisions and is waiting for a flash of inspiration.
- Management is counting on knowing a good rock when they see it.

- The decisionmaker has little respect for other people and their time.
- They are unaware of the ramifications of their request: the amount of time it will take and what projects will suffer from the lost time.
- They do not understand or is unaware of the frustration they cause.
- Rarely, they are just messing with you.

Conversations for Action are powerful for delegation and serve to transform possibilities into reality. When implemented well, the **Bring Me a Rock Game** never happens. The model sets the stage for delegation, accountability and pin-pointing the source of recurring problems that lower the performance bar in organizations.

In **Conversations for Action**, trust becomes super-relevant and provides the foundation for individuals working together. We establish trust through **Conversations for Relationship** and by proving consistency in delivering results from other **Conversations for Action**. Trust is expensive to build, so it helps to envision a compelling future together to make the investment worthwhile. As a note of caution, pick those whom you work with carefully. As my dear Irish mother would caution, "It is much easier to get them, then to get rid of them".

How do you get other people to do what you want? Begin by knowing what you want and form a precise vision of the outcome before you begin.

Communication is not so much about what you say as what the other person understands. You need to take responsibility for what you communicate. It is your responsibility to confirm their understanding, and if the other person doesn't get it, improve your explanation so they understand what you intended.

Conversations for Action are based on the complete atom of work.

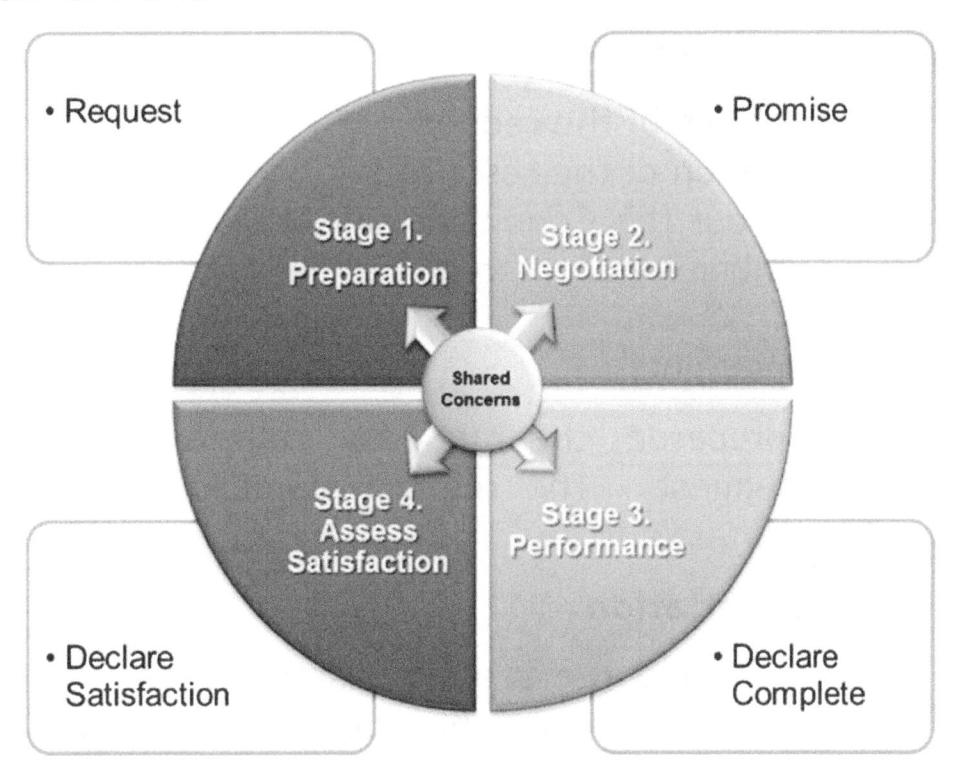

- Request
- Promise
- Declare Satisfaction
- Declare Complete

Stage 1. Preparation
Stage 2. Negotiation
Stage 3. Performance
Stage 4. Assess Satisfaction

Shared Concerns

The **Atom of Work** builds upon solid requests and promises. At the core resides a set of shared concerns between the person making the request and the one making the promise. The shared concerns could be as simple as both your jobs are dependent on delivering the result. When an interdependence exists and you need to cooperate to accomplish the goal or address the concern, **Conversations for Action** is the tool to use.

Stage 1: Preparation.

Prepare as complete a request as possible, with special emphasis on the conditions for satisfaction and timing. At times, there are no additional constraints nor resources. However, if constraints and resources become a factor, specify them during the preparation stage. Preparation includes:

- A description of the request
- Identification of the resources
- Spelling out the Conditions of Satisfaction so there is no ambiguity of the required deliverables
- Timing
- Any constraints

Once fully prepared, the requestor calls a meeting to make the request. The request signifies the end of Stage 1.

Stage 2: Negotiation

The person making the promise listens to the request and responds. There are only four options other than agreeing:

1. The promisor can negotiate the task, resources, Conditions of Satisfaction, timing, or constraints.

2. The promisor can make a counter-offer. They may see a different approach or offer an alternate set of

deliverables that may be better. The alternative approach must be agreeable to the requestor.

3. There may be a commitment to <u>commit later</u>. This often happens in matrix organizations where an individual has dotted line responsibility to others. A responsible individual ensures there are no conflicting obligations. The goal is a solid promise without contingencies. Therefore, check and clear contingencies before making the commitment.

4. The promisor may <u>decline</u>. This may be difficult when the requestor has positional power over the promisor. In these cases, the promisor may need to disagree and commit to the request anyway. Or the promisor may respond with "yes and" where what follows the "and" is the impact of saying yes. For example, "yes, I will deliver on the request as specified, and the work on the strategic initiative will be delayed by a week. Is this acceptable?"

Stage 2 is complete when the promisor makes a <u>firm</u> commitment. It must be a solid promise. Neither, "I'll see what I can do" nor "I'll give it a try" will suffice. Remember from Star Wars, during his training on the planet Dagobah, when Luke Skywalker, said, "all right, I'll try it" Yoda replied "No, try not. Do or do not, there is no try". We are looking for a firm commitment and if there is anything holding back this commitment, it needs discussion before Stage 2 is complete.

Once there is a confirmed promise, the promisor does the work or action in Stage 3. This work may spin-off additional atoms of work.

When the action is complete at the end of Stage 3 the promisor declares it complete. There are only three acceptable alternatives to the work being complete:

1. A <u>re-negotiation</u> of the promise. This happens when unforeseen complications emerge while fulfilling the promise or the initial request changes.

2. The promisor may <u>revoke</u> the promise. This may happen when circumstances beyond the promisor's control change. When this happens, the promisor must proactively communicate to the requestor in a timely manner. The requestor needs to then release the promise. Otherwise the promise is still in effect.

3. The requestor may decide to <u>cancel</u> request. This happens when priorities change as they do from time-to-time. When this happens, the requestor must proactively communicate to the promisor in a timely manner. The promisor should then confirm work will stop for now. Otherwise the promise is still in effect and may waste time completing tasks that are no longer a priority.

The cycle is not complete until the requestor, in Stage 4, assesses the work and acknowledges fulfilling the Conditions of Satisfaction to an acceptable level. If the Conditions of Satisfaction remain unmet, the requestor states this, reminds the promisor of the promise and holds the promisor accountable for making the promise good. "You have not yet delivered satisfactorily on your promise. How do you propose to make good on your word?" If promisor doesn't make good, it will result in a breach of trust and more profound consequences.

Successful completion leads to a declaration of satisfaction. The following diagram shows the lifecycle of a request organized in "swim lanes".

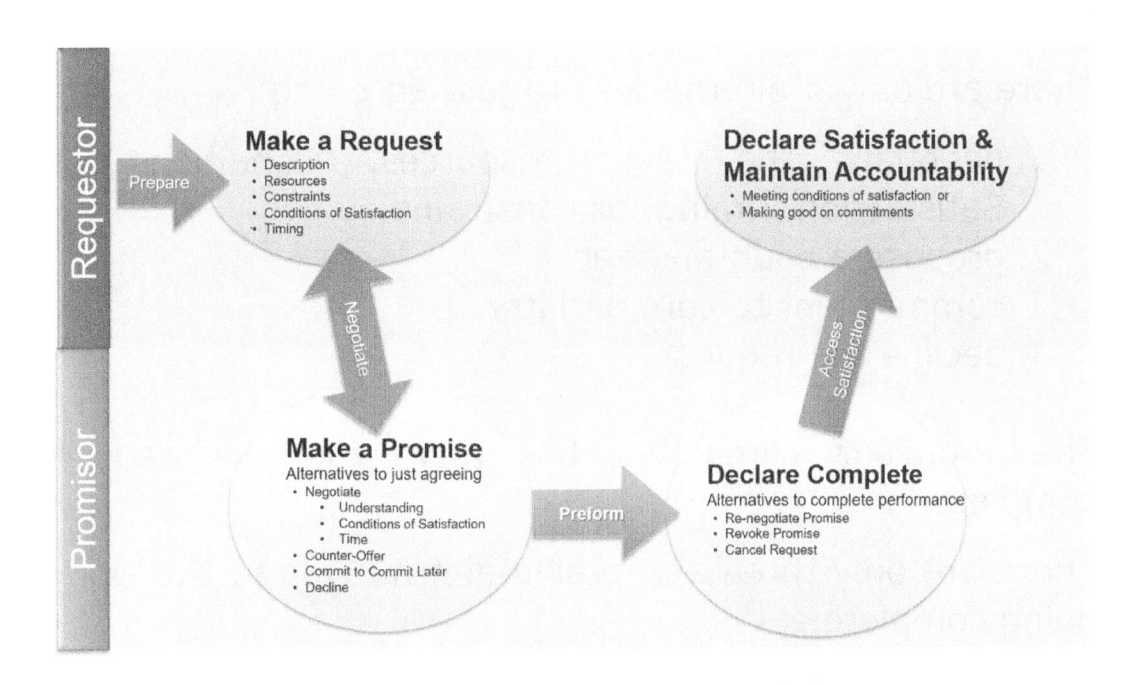

Requestor

Make a Request
- Description
- Resources
- Constraints
- Conditions of Satisfaction
- Timing

Prepare

Declare Satisfaction & Maintain Accountability
- Meeting conditions of satisfaction or
- Making good on commitments

Negotiate

Access Satisfaction

Promisor

Make a Promise
Alternatives to just agreeing
- Negotiate
  - Understanding
  - Conditions of Satisfaction
  - Time
- Counter-Offer
- Commit to Commit Later
- Decline

Preform

Declare Complete
Alternatives to complete performance
- Re-negotiate Promise
- Revoke Promise
- Cancel Request

Let's look at this from a process flow point of view.

There is a Requestor and Promisor, each has their own swim lane.

The Requestor gets prepared and makes a request:

The Request includes:

- a description
- the resources available
- any constraints
- the Conditions of Satisfaction and
- timing or timeframe

There is a negotiation between the Requestor and Promisor.

After full agreement, the Promisor makes a solid Promise.

There are only 4 alternatives to just agreeing:

1. negotiate the task, resources, Conditions of Satisfaction, timing, or constraints
2. propose a counter-offer
3. commitment to commit later
4. decline the request

The Promisor completes the task and declared it complete.

There are only three acceptable alternatives to the work being complete:

1. re-negotiation of the promise
2. Promisor revokes the promise
3. Requestor cancels the request

The **Atom of Work** is complete when the requestor assesses the work and declares satisfaction.

It is crucial for the Requestor to keep the Promisor accountable for their commitments. If the conditions remain unfulfilled, the Requestor must hold the Promisor accountable to make good on their commitments.

Let's keep two other ideas in mind:

1. One **Atom of Work** may spawn other atoms of work.
2. Breakdowns can occur at any place in the model. When a breakdown occurs, this model serves to diagnose what went wrong so that it doesn't continue to be a problem in future work.

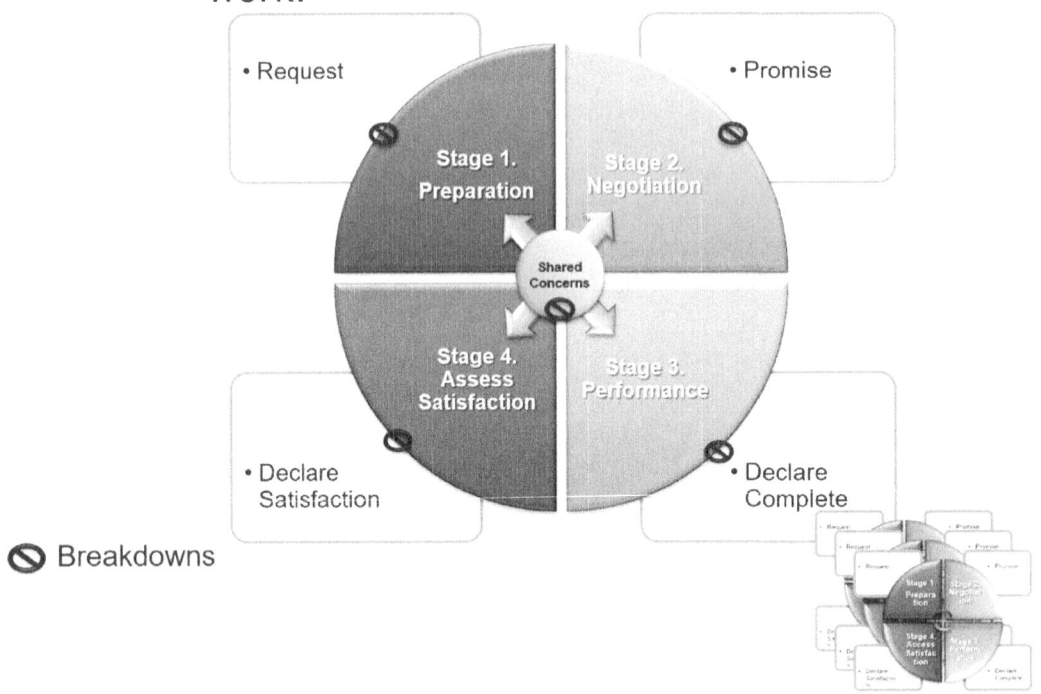

🚫 Breakdowns

Diagnosing Breakdowns

Using the model as a diagnostic tool is powerful. For any delegation that did not turn out well, use the model to find out what went wrong. You can assess the conversations across an entire department or organization using the **Atom of Work** model and determine where the breakdowns occur. This will guide you to get enough information to determine the root cause of the breakdown and insert preventive measures.

Stage 1				
Was there a clear and complete description of the request?	Yes☐	Partial☐	No☐	N/A☐
Were resources identified and made available?	Yes☐	Partial☐	No☐	N/A☐
Were the Conditions of Satisfaction specified so there is no ambiguity?	Yes☐	Partial☐	No☐	N/A☐
Was the timing specified?	Yes☐	Partial☐	No☐	N/A☐
Were constraints specified?	Yes☐	Partial☐	No☐	N/A☐
Stage 2				
Was there a solid promise?	Yes☐	Partial☐	No☐	N/A☐
Were negotiations complete?	Yes☐	Partial☐	No☐	N/A☐
Was there an acceptable counter offer?	Yes☐	Partial☐	No☐	N/A☐
Was any commitment to commit later followed up?	Yes☐	Partial☐	No☐	N/A☐
Was the request declined?	Yes☐	Partial☐	No☐	N/A☐
Stage 3				
Was the task completed?	Yes☐	Partial☐	No☐	N/A☐
Was the promise re-negotiated?	Yes☐	Partial☐	No☐	N/A☐
Was the request cancelled?	Yes☐	Partial☐	No☐	N/A☐
Was the work declared complete?	Yes☐	Partial☐	No☐	N/A☐
Stage 4				
Were the deliverables consistent with the request?	Yes☐	Partial☐	No☐	N/A☐
Were resources identified and made utilized?	Yes☐	Partial☐	No☐	N/A☐
Were the Conditions of Satisfaction met with acceptable quality?	Yes☐	Partial☐	No☐	N/A☐
Was the delivery on time?	Yes☐	Partial☐	No☐	N/A☐
Were constraints followed?	Yes☐	Partial☐	No☐	N/A☐
Shared Concerns				
Were the shared concerns acknowledged?	Yes☐	Partial☐	No☐	N/A☐
Were the shared concerns in alignment?	Yes☐	Partial☐	No☐	N/A☐

Conversations for Delegation

Conversations for Action, as described above are powerful for delegating assignments. However, this doesn't cover all situations. Do you ever find your reports filling your email inbox by "coping you on everything? Do you ever find your employees moving too far and too fast on projects without keeping you posted? Do you ever find your manager making decisions you should be handling? If you answered yes, improve the situation by having a Conversation for Delegation.

Using 4-Level delegation clarify how to handle various decisions and actions so that individuals know exactly where they have authority.

Level	Label	Decide or Recommend	Get Approval	Act	Report	Note
1	Just do it!	X		X		Make the decision, act and do not report. These are often daily activities expected with the job.
2	Do it & report	X		X	X	Make the decision, act, and report your action on a regular basis. These items are important for your manager to know and may show up on your performance review.
3	Get approval	X	X	-	-	Make the decision and get approval before acting. These are typical of issues that other parts of the organization.
4	Input only	X	-	-	-	Gather data and provide input to upper management so they can make an informed decision. Do not act until explicitly asked.

Conversations for Delegation

If you're a manager, gather your group to share this model. It is best to ask them to provide examples of each level of delegation so they participate and better internalize the boundaries and expectations. If they put a certain activity in the wrong level, tell them the right level and why.

Fully empower them to act on Level 1. There is no need to ask for permission nor to copy you in correspondence. This demonstrates your trust and confidence in them and gives the permission they need to act in confidence. It also serves to reduce the number of emails you currently receive.

For Level 2, be sure to specify the frequency you want to receive reports and the level of detail you expect.

At Level 3, let them know the best ways to contact you for approval. You may want an email with "Approval Needed" in the subject line or you may prefer another method. When it's best to have an audit trail rather than relying on verbal approvals, use email or text messages. In the right circumstances, a verbal approval can work.

For Level 4, you want them to gather data and provide a recommendation for others to reference when making the decision. Action should wait until instructed.

Consider holding a similar conversation with your boss. It helps establish boundaries so they are less likely to micro-manage you. If you have an agreement and they do micro-manage, it is easier to remind them of your prior agreement that you handle all Level 1 and 2 items independently. Remind them it will free their time to work on higher level, more important items only they can address.

Likely, you will notice positive side effects immediately after holding a conversation for delegation with your team. It tends to improve morale and improve productivity. People feel more confident in their actions when the expectations and boundaries are clear.

Conversations for Accountability

Have you found it difficult to hold someone accountable for their actions? You might feel sorry for them. You might cut them slack as they were lacking some skills. You may believe it was your fault.

Conversations for Accountability are about respectfully holding people accountable for what they have explicitly committed to do and have not fulfilled. You need to step up and hold the conversation when there are unfulfilled promises within agreed upon expectations. The spirit of this conversation is not about "getting back" at people. Rather, it's about taking care of your own personal dignity and about developing constructive relationships in personal and professional life.

Accountability is not simply taking on blame when things go wrong. Nor is it confessing guilt. Accountability is about delivering on commitments. It's a responsibility to deliver an agreed-upon outcome, not just a set of activities. It's taking the initiative and following-through to completion.

Leaders rely on the people who report to them to follow through on their commitments. The process of relying on and holding others accountable can be frustrating. Some leaders revert to "command and control," become micro-managers, interrogate their reports, plead and in some cases, yell.

None of that works as a sustainable practice. Getting angry and sharing your frustration with people when they fail to live up to their commitments is not a productive way to hold people accountable. It damages both motivation and performance.

Up Front

Set **clear expectations**. Creating a **Culture of Accountability** begins with holding effective Conversations for Action. This not only allows you to be clear in setting expectations, it also requires the other party to make a solid commitment. It is not reasonable to hold someone accountable for something they did not explicitly commit to doing.

Make assignments where a **Capability to Succeed** exists. One trait of the trust wheel we described earlier is **competence**. To get a realistic commitment from someone, you need to trust they can do the job, which includes having the skills to complete the task. Having someone take on a task when they do not have the skills potentially sets them up for failure. If they can't complete the task due to a lack of requisite skills, then you need to assign the task to someone else.

Establish **clear measurements and standards**. Measures and metrics become part of the Conditions of Satisfaction in Conversations for Action. For larger tasks, it's helpful to monitor progress at interim milestones. If progress starts to slip, you need an early warning to take corrective action before it's too late.

During and After

Provide **clear and timely feedback**. Straight-talk in the form of clear, honest, open, ongoing feedback is critical. People appreciate knowing where they stand. If you have clear expectations, capability and measurement, then feedback can be based on objective, observable facts. It's more important to be helpful with straight talk than it is to be nice and try to spare someone's feelings.

Provide an opportunity to **make things right**. Before jumping to consequences give the individual the opportunity to correct any problems or make up for what went wrong. This is not always possible nor appropriate. However, you will develop a better employee if they have the chance to make things right. It promotes respect and fairness.

Sometimes the down side of risk raises its ugly head. If the individual demonstrated best efforts on a risky project that did not go well, be soft and supportive of the individual. Coming down hard on someone when it is not their fault will kill morale, innovation and future risk-taking. Instead, ask what we can learn from the situation and examine alternate steps to minimize the impact of risk in the future.

Establish and follow through with **clear and appropriate consequences**. If you've done your part, you've done what's necessary to support their performance, so don't just take it on yourself with no consequences for others. Three healthy possibilities at the end of a task include:

1. **Reward and praise** if the individual succeeded.
2. Give the individual or someone else the opportunity to **repeat or correct** the tasks if you think they can now succeed.
3. **Reassign or release** individuals that consistently do not deliver or prove themselves as accountable, and you're confident you did your part. Their actions let you know they're not a good fit for the role, and you should reassign them or release them to explore the job market.

When you conduct **Conversations for Accountability**:

- It is about respectfully holding people accountable for what they have explicitly committed to do and have not fulfilled. Begin by visiting the specifics of the accountability:
    - The commitment made and when
    - The Conditions of Satisfaction including any metrics or deliverables and timing

- Focus on <u>what's</u> right or wrong, not <u>who's</u> right or wrong. It helps to focus on solutions versus focusing on blame.
- Lead with data and observable facts. Keep the emotions out of the conversation to the extent possible. Sometimes, emotions need acknowledgement before it is possible to continue with productive dialogue. Stick to the facts so it is about business results and not so personal. Strive for an elevated level of transparency.
- Declare the damage resulting from not fulfilling this commitment. For example, not being able to move on with other tasks or not being able to meet promises made to other people or damage to identity and performance.
- Be aware of individuals clever at avoiding accountability. Avoiding accountability can be a defense mechanism. An individual may fear accountability due to fear of messing things up and the imagined consequences. They may use a variety of techniques to avoid having the accountability fall back on them:
    - Avoid, reword, or repackage, the promise
    - Obfuscate the facts
    - Deflect the issue by talking about mistakes made by you or someone else
    - Rationalize and/or disguise any culpability
    - Claim to have delegated the matter to someone else internally
    - Do anything and everything to avoid a review

- Stonewall, gaslight, or come off as sarcastic and accusing

  The best advice is simply address the ploy openly and sincerely. Disarm the ploy by labeling the observed behavior. For example, if the ploy from your counterpart is stubborn unresponsiveness, one option is to candidly say, "I don't know how to interpret your silence."

- Give the individual the opportunity to correct the situation and make amends for any part of the problem they own. If the quality was poor, provide coaching and resources to improve the quality. When missing deadlines, consider extensions where possible or encourage additional effort on their part to make it right.
- Close as appropriate.
  - Reward and praise if the individual succeeded.
  - Give the individual or someone else the opportunity to repeat the tasks if you think they can now succeed.
- Reassign or release individuals that have not delivered or proven accountable if you're confident you did your part.

Accountability Assessment

Up Front	
Were clear expectations set in advance?	Yes☐ Partial ☐ No ☐ N/A☐
Was the individual capable of completing the task?	Yes☐ Partial ☐ No ☐ N/A☐
Were there clear measurements and standards?	Yes☐ Partial ☐ No ☐ N/A☐
Did they make a solid commitment?	Yes☐ Partial ☐ No ☐ N/A☐
During and After	
Did you provide clear and timely feedback?	Yes☐ Partial ☐ No ☐ N/A☐
Did the individual have an opportunity to make things right?	Yes☐ Partial ☐ No ☐ N/A☐
Were there clear and appropriate consequences?	Yes☐ Partial ☐ No ☐ N/A☐
Was praise given for success?	Yes☐ Partial ☐ No ☐ N/A☐

Conversations for Confrontation

Most people find themselves reluctant to hold conversations involving confrontation. Some of the top reasons individuals avoid **Conversations for Confrontation** include:

- Concern about causing upset
- Concern about stressing out the other person
- Stressing out themselves
- Recognition that expectations were not clear enough
- Concern about being fair
- Concern about short-term awkwardness in the relationship
- Concern about long-term or permanent damage to the relationship
- Concern about an angry response
- Issues left unaddressed for too long
- Hadn't gathered sufficient evidence to tackle the issue

The sooner you find the courage to step up and hold the conversation, the better for all parties. If you speak the truth from a space of caring and consideration, you provide the space for others to grow and prosper.

Successful **Conversations for Confrontation** require preparation and skill. Start by filling out the following prep form. When you write out the words, your brain processes the data differently and you're better able to see gaps.

Concisely state the heart of the issue in 1 or 2 sentences. There may be more than one underlying issue so be sure to call them out separately, on separate forms. The issue could be a concern, challenge, opportunity, or recurring problem that is becoming more of an issue.	The issue is...
What's at stake? How does this effect: the team, customers, goals, profits, loss, costs, products, services, suppliers, timing, the future, or other relevant factors? What does the future look like if it continues?	This is important because...
What are your emotions resulting from the issue? Emotions include: surprise, disappointment, anger, concern, etc. What is triggering this emotion? Does this surface yet another issue?	My emotions around this issue are...
What is your contribution to the issue?	I may have contributed by...
What is important to the other person? What is at stake for them and how might they react to your addressing the issue? How do you want to respond to their reactions?	They may respond with...
What specific results do I want? What are the observable changes necessary? If the issue was no longer present, what would a successful scenario look like?	An ideal outcome is...
Make a list of background facts detailing the who, what, when, where, why and how. What forces are in play; what is the status? This list will prepare you to address issues and potential push-back in the conversation.	Relevant background information...
What options are up for consideration?	The consequences of no notable change could include...
What are acceptable alternative solutions. Often there is more than one right answer. This is a list you keep in your hip pocket until it's needed.	Other acceptable solutions include...

Before you begin, get clear about your **desired outcome**. This will keep you grounded, focused and on-track in your conversation. It will also greatly improve getting the result you want and avoid unintended consequences.

Manage your presence by intentionally choosing your most effective mood, body posture, voice tonality, and facial expression. Consider what will work best for setting the stage, encouraging participation, and enhancing constructive listening. Remember to present yourself sincerely.

The first step when engaging in a **Conversation for Confrontation**, is **naming the issues**. When there are more than one serious issues, a good option is to identify all upfront and then discuss each major issue in detail one at a time. You may spend a lot of time on a single issue, be sure to circle back and address the others. If you don't cover everything in one meeting, identify what you intend to cover in the next meeting. However, **pick your battles**. You may not need to cover all the issues to get your desired outcome. It's often not productive to continue to hammer someone over small issues when you've successfully addressed the big issues.

Provide **specific examples** of the issues you're confronting. Ideally, these are observable or measurable data points based in fact. Avoid using hear-say evidence. If you do not have enough examples gathered, consider waiting to hold the conversation until you're better prepared.

Describe the **emotions**, if any, you have around the issue. Emotions may include surprise, disappointment, anger, concern, etc. Keep it real and don't avoid the emotional wake caused by the issue. If you do not experience any emotions about the issue, then leave this part out and don't feel compelled to invent something.

State **why each issue is important**. The issue may be important for several reasons. It will be your judgement on how much to share. If you pile on too much, it may detract from getting the desired outcome you seek and result in unintended consequences like devastating morale. As a rule, be as transparent as possible.

Identify **your contribution** in creating the issue. This doesn't mean falling on your sword and assuming all accountability. However, by stepping up to your contribution, you maintain integrity and create more of an opening for a successful outcome. Some difficult individuals may use this as an opportunity to deflect their accountability on to you. It is necessary for you to keep the focus on their contribution to the issue and the actions they need to take for a successful outcome.

Indicate your **desire to resolve** the issue. This can be a simple declarative statement and you should be able to move through this step quickly. Keep in mind that the other person may be on the defensive at this point and will be checking your sincerity. As a guideline, be as transparent as possible.

Invite the **other person to respond**. If you're lucky, they will acknowledge the issue, own their contribution, and commit to taking steps toward resolution. Those steps should include: correcting any resulting repercussions, and committing to not letting it happen again.

In some cases, the conversation will not go that smoothly. Be sure to use active listening to **confirm your understanding of their points**. Keep in mind their initial response will only be at the surface of the issue. Ask open-ended questions to **inquire for full understanding** until you expose the core of the issue. If necessary, walk through all the steps above starting with naming the issue and check for understanding and alignment on each point. This will **solidify areas of agreement** and identify areas of disconnect where you need to spend more time in conversation.

Once you get agreement on an acceptable outcome with identified next steps, recap and confirm that you're both on the same page for all points. Check the commitment of the other to following through. Spell out the **consequences** in advance if the issue continues.

Dealing with Emotions

Sometimes, the person you confront will have emotions well up in the form of emotional flooding or emotional hijacking. You may notice their face getting red, their skin blotching or their eyes may start tearing and they look away.

Help avoid emotional flooding by using "I" statements instead of "you" statements. "You" statements tend to trigger a defensive and potentially emotional response due to the judging nature of the delivery.

Staying specific will help you appear more objective and avoid emotional triggers. Over-generalizing takes the form of sweeping conclusions, abstractions, or labels, and using words like "always" and "never." These types of generalizations fuel the fear that can trigger an emotional response.

Compassion goes a long way in working through an emotional response. It can take the form of offering appreciations, praise, focusing on the positive, and sharing gratitude. Being unkind is likely to elicit the opposite reaction. Focusing on what's not working and what we don't like, throws a blanket on furthering a conversation and produces anger and feelings of distance or fear of attack in the other person.

Interrupt their pattern by using their name, asking a question, and then simply listening. That means seeking to truly understand what someone is saying, and encouraging their communication. This brings closeness and can diffuse their reaction. We all know how the opposite feels when we are vulnerable. Quick interruptions, debates, and wise-cracks don't truly acknowledge the speaker and instead make the situation worse.

Don't assume you need to terminate the conversation because someone has an emotional response. A little space goes a long way toward getting back on track.

Use your senses to determine if someone becomes swept up in sadness, anger, or fear. With practice, you will recognize the emotions underneath other's demeanor, words, and actions. Rather than directly reacting to what they say or do, extend a communication "link" to help shift their emotional state by offering what they need to hear, but they don't know how to request in the moment.

Emotion	Link	Goal
Sadness	Appreciation	Joy
Anger	Understanding	Love
Fear	Reassurance	Peace

To figure out what emotion is surfacing, notice where they focus their attention. Individuals feeling sadness may be thinking or speaking poorly of themselves. You might observe them as passive or clingy. They need sincere appreciation. In your interactions with them, convey the idea, "I think highly of you. You're great." Remind them of their strengths and contributions.

Individuals striking out in anger and spewing "you this" and "you that" with blame, negativity, and criticism often feel isolated and are in desperate need of understanding. They won't respond well to debates, lectures, or reprimands. The chances they'll hear your message are slim to none unless connect with them first. You need to hear them out without taking what they say personally. Focus on what's going on behind their angry words and let their ranting go in one ear and out the other. Tell them "I want to hear what you have to say" and just listen.

If an individual appears overwhelmed, anxious, or freaking out, chances are they have unexpressed fear stockpiled. They need honest and realistic reassurances. Comfort, soothe, and remind them everything is and will be all right. Other reassuring comments include: "We'll make our way through this together;" "I'm here;" "I'll take care of it;" or "You've done this successfully before."

When you notice overwhelming emotional flooding, take a break from the conversation. You may want to say, "Let's take a pause for a minute so you can collect yourself. We are not in a hurry." Give the other person the space and grace to get their emotions under control.

Learning to read facial expressions will give you a clue about what is going on emotionally for individuals. Sometimes these expressions present for a split second. The pictures below demonstrate expressions reflecting specific emotions. Dr Paul Ekman of the Paul Ekman Group offers training tools to improve your skills at correctly identify micro expressions during conversations. The tools are SETT – METT (Subtle Expressions Training Tool - Micro Expressions Training

Tool) The good news is that with practice, it's possible to rapidly improve your skills in reading emotions.

Happiness
- Crow's feet wrinkles
- Movement from muscles that orbit the eye
- Pushed up cheeks

Anger
- Eyebrows down and together
- Eye glare
- Narrowing of the lips

Surprise
- Eyebrows raised
- Eyes widened
- Mouth open

Fear
- Eyebrows raised and pulled together
- Raised upper eyelids
- Tensed lower eyelids
- Lips slightly stretched horizontally back to ears

Disgust
- Nose wrinkled
- Upper lip raised

Sadness
- Drooping upper eyelids
- Loosing focus in eyes
- Slight pull down of lip corners

Terminations

Sometimes the Conversation for Confrontation means

terminating an employee. These conversations need careful planning and should fully involve human resources. If you're the individual's supervisor, then it will likely fall on you to have the conversation with the employee. The best advice is keep it quick and very clear. Here is a systematic approach:

1. "Hello, (First Name). Come in and sit down. I've got some bad news for you." You want to immediately set the tone.
2. "As you know, [the reason for the termination.]" State the reason for the termination in one short sentence. The shorter the better; avoid long explanations or background.
3. "As a result, it is my duty to let you know that your employment with the company has been terminated as of today." Be sure to use the past tense, not "will be terminated." It's complete and not open for debate.
4. Be specific about what will happen next: pay, benefits, unused vacation time, references, outplacement, and so forth. Do this homework beforehand so the conversation is complete and efficient. You do not want to leave room and later loop back.
5. Close by thanking the person for their contributions to the company. Even if the termination is for deficient performance, everyone makes some contribution. Ending on a graceful note can avoid future problems.

Before you begin the termination conversation, fully prepare yourself to deal with all the questions that inevitably come up:

- Is this my last day?
- Can I say goodbye to everyone before I go?
- When should I leave?
- Can I clear out my desk?
- Will I receive severance pay? How much?
- What about the bonuses I was eligible for?
- What about accumulated sick leave or vacation time not taken?
- How long will my medical and insurance benefits continue?
- When will I receive my last paycheck?
- Am I eligible for unemployment insurance?
- Will you or the company provide employment references? What will you say if asked to provide a reference?
- What will you tell my coworkers and clients about my termination?
- When do I need to return company property such as a laptop, cell phone, and keys?
- What happens to my pension, profit sharing, or 401K plans?
- Can I continue to use my work area to look for a job?

The termination meeting should be very brief, keep it to ten minutes or less. In your discussion, don't attempt to justify or defend the decision. This will help you keep it short and to the point. Stick to what you know for sure, just the facts. Make sure the person has heard the termination news clearly and avoid all personal attacks, accusations, or justifications. Don't tell the employee that this is difficult for you. Keep it all about them. If you handle the conversation well, both of you will get over it faster.

An expedient conversation may leave them in a state of shock as you escort them out of the building. Consider coordinating with your IT department to begin changing passwords and terminating all access while you hold the termination meeting. Someone else can be packing their personal items. You do not want to give a disgruntled employee the opportunity to send unfortunate emails, seek revenge, or steal key data as they head out.

Conversations for Selling

In business, we constantly sell. Sometimes we sell products or services to external customers and other times we sell our ideas internally. In either case, results improve when you raise quality of your Conversations for Selling.

First, let's distinguish selling from order taking. Selling refers to a relational event, and order taking is more transactional. When engaged in transactional order taking, it's most important to follow the flow for Conversations for Action. Including relational elements is still important in transactional order taking. The relational elements become important when you try to turn a one-off transaction into a repeat customer or a positive reference.

Conversations for Selling represent a flow of conversation types, starting with Conversations for Relationship that build rapport and trust; followed by Conversations for Possibility to discover needs and explore options; transitioning to Conversations for Action to agree on the terms, deliverables; and concluding with Conversations for Relationship to close on a good note and a bright future.

```
       Conversation for
         Relationship
              ↓
       Conversation for
          Possibility
              ↓
       Conversation for
            Action
              ↓
       Conversation for
         Relationship
```

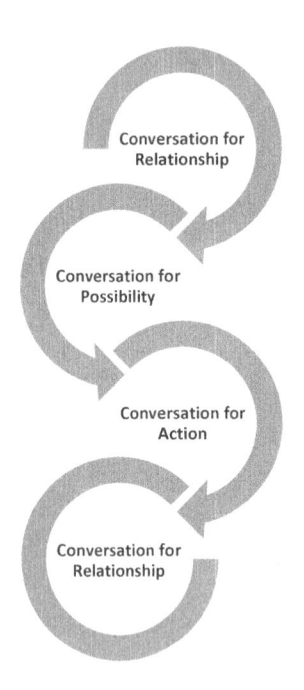

Conversations for Selling represent an advanced communication skill. This section lands at the end of the book because it builds on all the preceding principles and types of conversations.

Relationship selling

Other authors write extensively on relationship selling. The topic will not be covered in detail. Suffice it to say, relationship selling is about building a friendship or relationship with prospects and listening to their needs. Once you've built that relationship with a prospect and earned their trust, you're on the way to making them a long-term customer.

The largest part of making a purchase decision is based on an emotional reaction to the offering. The purchaser will often evaluate logically and then place a weighting on the selection criterion to support the emotional desire. Knowing your prospect's needs and finding out their related fears can help you find solutions for them that are exactly on-target with their emotional and business needs.

It is possible to leverage and even improve a strong relationship when things go wrong. With a strong relationship in place, working out details or dealing with issues is much easier. Without a strong relationship smaller issues can become insurmountable obstacles.

Speak the Language of the Buyer

Especially for big ticket items, there are distinct roles for buyers, each with their own unique focus. Sometimes, multiple roles reside in one person. In many cases, they're spread across several specialists. The **financial buyer** is interested in the costs and financial returns and expects you to communicate in economic terms. The **end user's** concern is with the functionality. The **technical buyer** needs to know the specifications and how the item plays with other systems. For personal domestic purchases, often the complete buying unit consists of both spouses. Be sure to view the world through each of their perspectives and speak in terms they can relate to.

Use the platinum rule instead of the golden rule. The Golden Rule reads "Do unto others as you would have them do unto you." The Golden Rule implies the basic assumption that other people prefer to be treated the way that <u>you</u> would like to be treated. The alternative is the Platinum Rule: "Treat others the way <u>they</u> want to be treated.

Keep in mind that the customers vote with their dollars and you want those votes cast in your direction. Focus on relating well, expressing the benefits to your customer and treating them as they want to be treated.

Explore the "we" space

It can be tempting to jump into selling features, benefits, or problem-solving. However, it's best to first establish some rapport. As we mentioned earlier in Conversations for Relationship, start by exploring the "we" space. Small talk, when done well, treats the other as a valued individual deserving of your honor. Once you've established some common ground, then discover more about their world and concerns.

Identify the Gaps

Engage in a discovery process by asking open ended questions to identify the gap between their current state and their desired state. Identify current problems, opportunities, constraints, wants, or needs. More effectively find a solution just right for them by identifying where they are and where they want to be. Moreover, as you engage and really listen, you build trust and rapport. The discovery process is a wonderful time to demonstrate your caring by taking the time to understand them.

Conversations for Selling

Explore possibilities

Once you know their situation and needs, begin exploring possibilities. Begin with what they think is the right approach and build from there. Keep in mind that you continually set expectations in the mind of the customer. Be conscious of this as the customer's ultimate satisfaction is a function of the alignment between what they <u>need</u>, what they <u>expect</u> and what they <u>receive</u>. If any of these elements are not in alignment, then customer dissatisfaction will result.

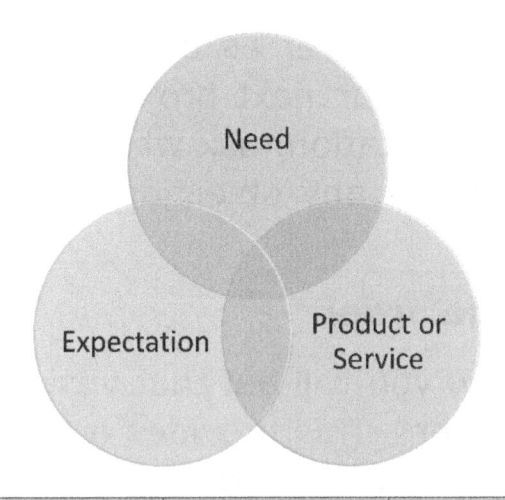

	Dissatisfaction	Dissatisfaction	Dissatisfaction	Satisfaction
Need	Aligned	Aligned	Not Aligned	Aligned
Expectation	Aligned	Not Aligned	Aligned	Aligned
Product or Service	Not Aligned	Aligned	Aligned	Aligned

For example, if there is little overlap in the intersection of what the customer **needs**, what they **expect** and the product or service they **receive**, then there will be

137

high dissatisfaction or low value in the mind of the customer.

Maximize the alignment between what the customer needs, what they expect and what you deliver. This will maximize customer satisfaction and lead to your success.

Make a selection

Once you have determined there is alignment, articulate the offering to the customer so they can make a final selection. Surface any objections to closing the sale by using a "trial close". A trial close asks, "if we can deliver as described, would you use this solution for your next project?" If the answer is no or there is hesitation, ask what it would take to get to a yes? Address any objections and repeat the trial close.

Asking for the order

Once you know you will get that yes, it is necessary to ask for the order. This provides a clear declaration of agreement and give you the green light to complete the sale.

Complete the sale

In this final stage, reconfirm the details for fulfillment which might include the who, what, and when aspects of the fulfillment.

Index

"

"I" Statements 125
"We" Space 65, 136
"You" Statements 39, 125

4

4-Level Delegation 112

A

Accountability 21, 57, 64, 100, 102, 115, 117, 118, 120, 124
Acknowledge 56
Actions 45
Advocating 47, 49, 50, 51, 75
Agreement 81
Amelia Earhart 19
Anger 39, 122, 124, 126, 127
Asking 18, 27, 38, 41, 49, 53, 66, 71, 72, 80, 92, 96, 136
Assertions 98, 99
Assumptions 42, 43, 44, 45, 46, 52, 53, 56, 83, 84
Atom Of Work 103, 110
Attitude 21, 22, 23, 68, 71
Authentic 38, 65, 67, 84
Avoid Conflict 25, 83

B

Bad Attitude 22
Balancing Advocacy And Inquiry 51, 52, 53
Be Direct 36

139

Index

Be Intentional 18
Be Present 14, 17, 18, 79
Behind Yourself 18
Beliefs 38, 42, 43, 44, 45, 56
Bil Keane 17
Blame 11, 32, 49, 56, 76, 114, 117, 127
Body Language 68, 69
Brains 42
Brainstorming 9, 90, 93
Breakdown 110, 111
Bring Me A Rock 101, 102
Building Rapport 76

C

Cancel 106, 108
Cancer 22, 74
Capability 115, 116
Caring 18, 37, 71, 72, 75, 136
Champion 18, 96
Chaos 81
Character 14, 71, 72
Choice .... Vi, 22, 32, 41
Choices 27, 44
Choose The Participants 10
Clarifying Questions 18
Clear Expectations 115, 116, 120
Close The Loop 58
Closed-Ended Questions 69
Command And 23
Commitment 21, 105, 108, 111, 115, 117, 118, 120, 125
Communication In Groups 81
Community 82
Compassion 71, 72
Competence 70, 72, 115
Conclusions 45

140

Conditions Of Satisfaction.......... 59, 104, 106, 108, 111, 116, 117
Confirm 59
Confront 19, 125
Consequences 15, 19, 49, 99, 107, 116, 117, 118, 120, 122, 123, 124, 125
Consistency 57, 70, 72, 102
Conversations For Accountability 114
Conversations For Action 64, 97, 100, 102, 103, 104, 112, 115, 116, 133
Conversations For Confrontation 64, 100, 121
Conversations For Delegation 64, 100
Conversations For Possibility 86
Conversations For Relationship 63, 65, 133
Conversations For Selling 65, 100, 133, 134
Costs 122, 135
Courage 15, 18, 19, 47, 48, 49, 70, 71, 72, 75, 121
Create A Safe Environment 13
Creativity 21
Credibility 70

D

Dealing With Disagreement 55
Declarations 98, 99
Decline 105, 108
Desired Outcome 11, 18, 81, 123, 124
Diagnosing 110
Dilemmas 27, 28
Direct 36, 37, 38
Discovery 80
Discovery Conversations 9
Distinguish Facts From Meaning 39
Dr Paul Ekman 128

E

Edge 21

141

Ego 39
Embarrassment 38, 48
Emotional Flooding 125, 128
Emotions 35, 49, 50, 52, 84, 117, 122, 124, 125, 127, 128
Empathy 37, 68, 70, 71, 72, 77, 80
Empower 113
Emptying 81
Energy 21
Enroll 95
Enthusiasm 21
Expectations 12, 101, 113, 114, 115, 121, 137
Explaining 27, 32, 49, 51, 96
Eye Color 68
Eye Contact 35, 60, 68

F

Fact 28, 38, 40, 42, 88, 123
Fear 19, 38, 48, 49, 118, 126, 127, 128
Feasibility 92
Feedback 70, 77, 116, 120
Feelings 20, 33, 34, 36, 37, 38, 39, 48, 83, 116, 126
Follow Through 59
Frame 22, 23, 24, 25, 26, 27, 28

G

Gaps 136
Generating 64, 87, 88, 90
Give Up Control 22, 25
Going Along To Get Along 19
Ground Rules 13, 14, 15, 17, 83, 84, 90
Group Rapport Building 78

H

Hands Off 25

Honest 37, 38, 57, 76, 84, 116, 128

I

I See You 66
Ideation 87, 88
Imagination 21
Impasse 56
Improving 91
IMS 93
Inconvenience 38
Inferences 42
Innovation Across And Organization 87
Inquiry Questions 54
Integrity 15, 26, 27, 39, 48, 50, 57, 71, 76, 124
Intention 21
Intentions 18, 31, 32, 34
Interrupt 126
Invite 124

J

Jerks 37

K

Kanji Symbol 35
Keeping Confidences 15

L

Label 29, 32, 112
Ladder Of Inference 32, 42, 45
Language Of Report 66, 74
Left-Hand Column 29, 30, 32, 33, 34
Link 127
Listen 34, 75, 80, 84

143

Index

Lose Face 48
Love 18, 37, 75

M

Maintain Integrity 47
Make Things Right 116, 120
Meaning 31, 40, 41, 42, 49
Measurements And Standards 116, 120
Mechanisms 21
Micro-Manage 113
Mindset .... Vi, 11, 12, 21, 22, 26, 27, 28, 30, 31, 34, 36, 80
Motives 23, 25, 27, 34
Mutual Learning 22, 26, 27, 28, 32, 50, 51

N

Name The Issues 123
Needs 71, 101, 105, 106, 133, 134, 135, 136, 137, 138
Negotiation 104, 106, 108
Ngikhona 66

O

Observe 43, 127
One-On-One Meetings 10, 15
Open Ended Questions 27, 36, 69, 80, 81, 125, 136
Overarching Principles Vi

P

Paraphrase 31
Performance 21, 63, 97
Personal Growth 19
Pick The Venue 9
Pick Your Battles 123
Pitfalls 33

Pool Of Available Data 45
Poor Performance 8
Possibilities .... Vi, 64, 87, 90, 99, 102, 117, 137
Possibility 21, 63, 64, 89, 97, 133
Posting 9
Preparation 8, 104, 121
Presence 17, 123
Principle 18, 27
Pringles 88
Prioritization 92
Prioritizing 9, 64, 87
Problem19, 22, 26, 30, 33, 34, 43, 50, 88, 89, 92, 110, 119, 122, 136
Productive 8, 15, 29, 34, 49, 73, 82, 83, 84, 115, 118, 123
Promises 76, 98, 100, 103, 114, 118
Promisor 107
Pseudo-Community 81, 83

Q

Quality Of The Conversation 9
Questions 45

R

Rapport 63, 65, 66, 74, 76, 78, 80, 133, 136
Rationale 27
Reinforcing Loop 43, 45
Relating 80
Relationship 21, 63, 65, 68, 76, 80, 81, 97, 102, 133, 134, 136
Relationship Selling 134
Report 66, 112, 115
Request 59, 100, 103, 104, 105, 106, 107, 108, 111
Requestor 107
Requests 98, 100
Responsibility 21, 31, 103, 105, 114
Results 21, 63

145

Revoke 106, 108
Reward And Praise 117, 119
Risk 14, 19, 30, 33, 70, 72, 74, 83, 101, 116

S

Sadness 127
Safety Net 13, 14, 15, 17
Sawubona 66
SCAMMPER Method 91
Selected "Data" 45
Selecting Data 31
Selfish 38
Set 94, 115
Set The Stage 8, 123
SETT – METT 128
Shared Concerns 111
Showing Up 16, 18, 19, 51
Solution 19, 53, 93, 94, 95, 96, 136
Solution Selection 93
Specific Examples 123
Spirit 21
Stakeholders 10
Star Wars 105
Success 8, 9, 27, 68, 120, 138
Swim Lanes 107

T

Take Control 22, 23, 24
Terminations 129
Thinking 21
Threshold Of Our Lips 48
Tie-Off 60
Too Much Information (TMI) 74
Trust 15, 37, 38, 45, 67, 68, 69, 70, 71, 72, 73, 74, 75, 100, 102, 107, 113, 115, 133, 134, 136

Trust Wheel 72, 73, 115
Truth 18, 37, 39, 48, 57, 75, 83, 99, 121
Truthful 38, 72

U

Upset 8, 31, 38, 52, 121

V

Velocity .... Vi, 8, 16, 34, 49, 65
Viewpoint 27

Y

Yo-One 61
Your Contribution 122, 124

Made in the USA
Middletown, DE
16 September 2025